THE Children's Writer's *Reference*

Berthe Amoss & Eric Suben

WRITER'S DIGEST BOOKS
CINCINNATI, OHIO

Other fine Writer's Digest Books are available from your local bookstore or direct from the publisher.

Visit our Web site at www.writersdigest.com for information on more resources for writers.

To receive a free weekly E-mail newsletter delivering tips and updates about writing and about Writer's Digest products, send an E-mail with "Subscribe Newsletter" in the body of the message to newsletter-request@writersdigest.com, or register directly at our Web site at www.writersdigest.com.

03   02   01   5   4   3   2

Library of Congress Cataloging-in-Publication
Suben, Eric.
   The chidren's writer's reference / by Eric Suben and Berthe Amoss.
     p.   cm.
   Includes biographical references.
   ISBN 0-89879-904-X (alk. paper)
   1. Children's literature—Authorship Handbooks, manuals, etc. 2. Children—Books and reading Handbooks, manuals, etc. I. Amoss, Berthe. II. Title.
PN147.5.S82   1999
808.06′8—dc21   99-43141
                                                                          CIP

Editors: David Borcherding, Michelle Howry and Alice Pope
Designer: Angela Lennert Wilcox
Cover illustrator: Kathleen Kinkopf
Production coordinator: Kristen D. Heller

About the Authors

Berthe (pronounced *bear-t*) Amoss is the author and/or illustrator of numerous picture books and young-adult novels. She taught children's literature at Tulane University for twelve years, during which time she also wrote a column on children's books for *The Times-Picayune*. She is in charge of product development for More Than A Card, Inc., a card and book publishing company.

Eric Suben, now a practicing attorney, was formerly editor-in-chief of Golden Books and director of the Children's Book Council. He has been a frequent panelist and lecturer on children's publishing, has written articles on the subject, and is the author of more than twenty-five picture books for young children.

The authors have collaborated in teaching courses at Tulane and a series of day-long workshops. Their advice comes from extensive professional experience, intensive work with students, and familiarity with the issues of greatest concern to students. The unique writing and illustrating exercises presented in this book were developed for these classes and workshops. Students and workshop participants at all levels have used the exercises to draw insights into their own work and help build needed skills.

Table of Contents

Introduction

If you want to write for children, this book will give you the information you want when you want it. Perhaps you are just starting your book and need some general ideas to get your creative juices flowing. Maybe you are stuck at a critical turning in the plot and need that one special detail to jog your story loose. If you pick up this book and turn to the appropriate chapter, you will find a wealth of ideas to inspire you and move your story along.

This is a book of lists. Ideas to inspire or nudge you are strung together with related concepts. Think of each list as a menu. Choose what you want or what you need. It may be good for your story. If not, come back and choose again.

Although the lists are the main thing, they are not the only thing. We have years of experience in writing and publishing children's books, and we have distilled much of this experience into the text that introduces each chapter and list. Take advantage of our words of advice! A proper orientation will make each list that much more useful for you.

As we say repeatedly throughout this book, your children's book is like a movie and you are the director. You have the first and final say about every detail—not just the big things like characters and plot, but things like clothes, lighting, props. If you are writing a picture book, you must be able to visualize every aspect of your book. When writing longer fiction for older children, your ability to evoke sights, sounds and smells through words must be even greater. Browsing through this book will help you consider the details you haven't even thought about. The lists present you with options for filling in the blanks in your thinking and story.

It is important you not stop with our lists as presented. Let our lists inspire you. A word or phrase may shake loose the realistic memory or flight of fancy that gives your story wings. If you don't find the exact notion you need in our lists, use them as a jumping-off place to start theme-based lists of your own. The most important thing is to keep writing. This book is a friend to keep by your writing desk and call on when needed. It can give you that extra idea, that little note of encouragement to keep going.

Most of this book concerns itself with specifics of writing for children—character, plot, setting and so on. In the first chapter, we provide an overview of just what and who children are. One of the first earmarks of a professional in this field is a realistic understanding of children as both characters and audience and how they grow.

Chapter One

Children and Books

If you are a children's book writer, you want to write for children. Chances are, you also want to write *about* children. But children are a diverse group with widely differing skills, abilities and interests. Many factors impact the variations among children, but no factor counts more than the age of the child for whom or about whom you wish to write. Age impacts other aspects of a child's experience as well—appearance, psychology, emotions and world view. Here is a list of aspects to consider that may vary by age:

height	self-oriented/other-oriented
weight	mobility
size	locomotion
hair	financial resources
teeth	emotional resources
muscles	dependence/independence
motor coordination	altruism
motor skills	selfishness
reading	idealism
writing	activism
arithmetic	socializing
music	sexuality

In this chapter, we'll define just who are the children for whom and/or about whom you're writing. As a writer, you must have a clear idea of the age of your ideal reader. Also, you must be able to visualize your child characters in concrete terms. What do they look like? Think about size, both height and girth. Think about hair color, skin color, eye color and body type:

Hair Color

brown	gray
blond	honey blond
red	ash blond
auburn	silver blond
white	chestnut
black	blue-black

Skin Color

tan	dark brown
bronze	light brown
copper	fair
pale	olive
swarthy	café au lait

Eye Color

blue	black
green	violet
hazel	gray

Body Type

plump	stout
pudgy	fat
slim	tall
sleek	short
wiry	round-shouldered
stocky	erect

Clothing and shoes are key, as well as hairstyles and accessories. Younger children may wear some or all of the following styles:

diaper	socks
underwear	knit cap
playsuit	sweater
sunsuit	clothes with animal ears/faces
swimming trunks	baseball cap

stadium coat

mittens

sneakers

Mary Jane shoes

Doctor Denton pajamas

crew cut

buzz cut

ponytail

pigtails

braids

bangs

For preteens and young adults, fashion and even makeup may be part of the picture:

designer jeans

team T-shirts/sweatshirts

baggy pants

boxer shorts

sweat socks

running shoes

suit

tie

prom gown

leggings

platform shoes

shoes with chunky heels

platform sneakers

tank top

scrunchee

barrettes

lipstick

nail polish

hair gel/mousse

eye shadow

deodorant

shaving cream/lotion

Are the children in school? Answering this question will make you think hard about the children's ages and skills. You will know whether they can read and write and count. Maybe they are still finger painting and going on nature walks. How do they get to school? Do they have nap time and snack time? What about recess? Is it outdoors in a playground? What kind of teacher do the children have? Is there music in the classroom? Here is a spectrum of school activities, ranging from those done by the youngest children to those done by young people in the elementary grades and beyond.

reading

finger painting

writing

nap time

snack time

recess

spelling

counting

arithmetic

cursive writing

creative writing

book reports

show-and-tell

caring for classroom plants/animals

music time

rhythm band

computer skills

research

drawing

cutting and pasting

science experiments

nature walks

foreign languages

school plays

marching band

choir

school newspaper

team sports

What can they do now? Walking and talking are early milestones. What about dressing themselves, brushing their teeth, tying their shoes? Can the child ride a tricycle? A bicycle? What new tasks do they aspire to? What feelings do they have? How do they relate to the world? These are some of the most basic questions you should ask yourself about your reader or character, and they are questions you should try to be able to answer. Here is another spectrum of attributes, youngest to oldest, to help you imagine your character and/or your audience:

smiling

rolling over

picking up head

crawling

standing

first words

walking

talking

sorting

counting

adding/subtracting

letters

word recognition

reading

using the potty

brushing teeth

washing self

dressing self

tying shoes

riding a tricycle

using training wheels

riding a bicycle

organized games

music lessons

team sports

driving

How can you know all these things about your readers and your characters—how they look, dress and behave? One good way is to observe children in their everyday haunts. Children go to most of the same places as adults—remember to observe them as you go about your daily business. These days there are far fewer strictures on where parents will take their children. This means more opportunities for observation. Below is a list of places to observe children to make you aware of the need and opportunity to observe children wherever you go:

home	theater
school	restaurant
playground	church/synagogue
city bus	store
street	mall
day care	party
park	museum
subway	

Watch what they do, listen to how they talk, see how they dress. Watch for these factors:

slang
jokes
clothes picked by parents
clothes picked by children
shoes
hair
accompanied by parents/accompanied by peers
interaction with the opposite sex
carrying toys/books
means of locomotion (bike/in-line skates/skateboard)

Another key to making accurate observations about children is to think back to your own childhood. Although you may want your book to be an accurate reflection of the world today, the emotional truth of your story will resonate from what you can incorporate from your own internal experience as a young person. Get in touch with the following factors:

first words
first steps
transitional objects (blankie, toy animal)
imaginary friends
night fears/nightmares
sibling issues

preschool experience
starting school
childhood illnesses
first teeth/losing teeth
dressing self/tying shoes
riding a bicycle/tricycle
doctor/dentist visits
family gatherings
pets
holiday celebrations
friendships
family relationships
first experience of death
neighborhood
playing games/sports
losing/finding things
helping/chores/taking responsibility

Another good way to get in touch with children is to read lots of children's books. See how another author or illustrator has depicted children at different ages and see what clues tell the reader the age of the book's characters.

In the sections that follow, children are introduced in very rough age categories. Of course, individual children differ and develop at different rates. You may wish to depict a character who walks and talks a bit earlier or later than the norm. Your child character may be slow to separate from his parents or to dispense with a transitional object (e.g., a "blankie" or beloved stuffed animal). Your child characters should be convincing human beings, individuals and not automata constructed from the following very approximate blueprint. Rather, the categories should provide you with a map to help you know where you, your readers, and your characters are in terms of average development and expectations.

INFANT (BIRTH–ONE YEAR)

There are differing schools of thought about the appropriateness of books for the youngest of infants. It is a milestone when a baby becomes able to lift its head. Before that milestone is reached, there may not be much need for a book for an infant, as the muscular minimum to look and focus the gaze is not yet developed.

Books for infants are often printed and published in special formats that take into account infants' special qualities and needs. Infants often spit up, so books printed on plastic pages that wipe clean are welcome. Teething babies chew most things that come into their grip, so parents look for nontoxic inks and durable pages. Babies also lack the motor coordination needed to keep from poking themselves with sharp corners, so many baby books are printed on soft cloth pages. Books with heavy board pages frequently have rounded corners. There are puffy waterproof books that float in the tub. One clever individual had the idea for "key-ring books," similar to the chunky plastic key-ring toys babies enjoy, but with heavy board pages rather than plastic keys attached to the ring.

The Growing Tree program published by HarperCollins illustrates the variety of formats and subject areas appropriate for the youngest children. This program is graded by children's ages and features board books as well as books in more traditional formats. Topics for infants include animal sounds, daily routine and games babies like to play.

There are not many famous books for children in this age category. The most popular subject areas are Mother Goose, peekaboo and books about baby's activities or daily routine. Dorothy Kunhardt's *Pat the Bunny* is probably the most famous of books for very young children, but even this simple "touch-and-feel" book may be beyond the ken of infants. Margaret Wise Brown's *Goodnight Moon* or other books with simple, rhythmic text may be good read-to books, as the patterned words may have the same soothing effect as a lullaby.

This audience may not offer the writer a great deal of scope. However, infants are often characters in books for older children, so it is good to understand their attributes and their world. Infants may figure in any story about family life and also in stories about growing up and independence. Here are a few examples, ranging in age from youngest to oldest, of book types that might feature infant characters:

bedtime
bath time

mealtime
nap time
outing
motor skills (putting in/taking out; sorting)
finger rhymes
new baby in the family
when you were a baby
adoption story
family gathering story (holiday theme or other)
helping mother/father
where babies come from (nonfiction)
older child raising younger child
baby-sitting job
teenage pregnancy/motherhood
pet story (pampered pet displaced by new baby, e.g., *Lady and the Tramp*)

In this age category, children are largely passive and nonverbal. Their world is focused mostly on self, secondarily on family and home, with the mother or other primary caregiver looming very large. Children in this category are essentially helpless in terms of feeding or cleaning themselves and have little or no independent locomotion until they begin crawling and walking. However, infants increasingly enter the world outside the home as they start day care after several weeks or months of life. The primary characters in their world are themselves, their families and nonparental caregivers. Infants may see other infants but often do not show a particular interest in others, being still involved in their own needs.

Physical Characteristics

plump   no or few teeth
sparse hair   dimples and creases in skin

Milestones

smiling   raising head
teething   rolling over

sitting up	crawling
weaning	standing

Physical Abilities

see	sleep/wake
hear	splash
smell	scream
make sounds	cry
limited crawling	turn head
coo	distinguish among people
roll over	suck
smile	reach
hold up head	pick up
drool	stand (older)
blow bubbles	put things in mouth
cry	gaze
teethe	blink
grasp	burp

Infant Feelings

passive	tired
colicky	hurt
hungry	

Services Caregivers Provide

bathe	carry
dress	dandle
nurse	play with
feed	change
lift	toss in air
hold	

Clothing

diapers	shirts with snaps
plastic pants	bunting

receiving blanket   bonnet
cap   booties

Objects in Baby's World

mobile   pacifier
ball   rattle
crib   carriage
playpen   stroller
high chair   backpack/front pack
baby swing   bike seat
stacking rings   night-light
cloth books   blanket
plastic books   stuffed animal
car seat/seat belt   music box

Places in Baby's World

bathtub   backpack
crib   front pack
playpen   doctor's office
mommy and daddy's bed   parent's arms/lap
car seat   daddy's shoulders
bike seat

TODDLER (ONE YEAR–THREE YEARS)

Toddlers are young children who are learning to pull themselves upright, stand and walk. Their new mobility gives them a wider world and more interests, and this age is marked by curiosity, increased social and verbal skills and greater self-awareness. As an audience for books, toddlers have an increasing ability to follow simple plots and relate to basic learning concepts.

Many developmental milestones occur during this period in a child's life. In addition to walking, the child begins to express himself in words. Putting names to things is an important and delightful part of the child's learning during this period (although not, perhaps, as important to the child as touching things and even placing things in his mouth). The child also completes teething and becomes potty trained. The latter experience may be fraught with frustrations for parent and child and is certain to arouse strong emotions in the child. Bathroom topics have become increasingly popular as subject matter for simple picture books. So have other "gross" subjects formerly taboo. Here is a list of such topics that have grown increasingly acceptable in books for toddlers and slightly older children:

urination	scabs
defecation	foot odor
toilet flushing	body odor
flatulence	vomit
snot	

An only child is likely to become a sibling during early childhood years. This experience is almost certain to produce an emotional upheaval in the firstborn's life. The results may be powerful feelings of jealousy, dependence on the parents, independence from the parents, desire or willingness to nurture and teach, need to share and exhibit friendliness. This powerful experience is one of the classic picture-book topics.

Also during this time the child is apt to increase his involvement with the world as an independent social being. He may spend longer hours at day care or prenursery or prekindergarten programs. Diminishing passivity and increasing mobility, activity and curiosity lead to attachments to other children, teachers or other caregivers, and passionate exploration of the world around. At the early stages of toddlerhood, the child may only be able to watch older children play; as he grows older, he begins to join in himself. At first, the child may be passive around other children; at other times, aggressive.

The child is beginning to experience the anxiety that accompanies separation from the parents. The desire to explore the world may be accompanied by fear of the loss of contact and dependence on parents. This anxiety may express itself in a variety of ways, including sleeplessness or reluctance to go to or stay at preschool.

The child may become prone to mark up walls or books, remove the contents of cabinets and bookshelves, and generally wreak havoc in the house. Toddlers may also embarrassingly do similar things in the homes of others. This is also a time of increased dangers, as children remain low to the ground even while becoming mobile. Thus, hazards like fingers in light sockets may be most threatening at this time.

A crucial and famous period during this phase is the "terrible twos." Two-year-olds express their increasing independence by saying no, by deliberately refusing to go along with the parents' expressed wishes and desires. The child in this age range is in the throes of exploring the world and is not thinking about the consequences of his actions.

Books published for children in this age range include chunky board books, illustrated with photographs or realistic illustrations. Board books of all kinds are popular, partly because they can stand up to chewing and can be wiped clean of many kinds of mess. Books die-cut into shapes are popular, as well as books with stickers or other activities that children with more developed motor skills can enjoy. Simple picture books featuring word patterns, repetition of refrains and/or incidents, and simple plots all work beautifully for this age group. Simple folktales, rhymes and songs ("The Wheels on the Bus," "The Teddy Bears' Picnic") may provide the basis for such books; original books like Margaret Wise Brown's *The Runaway Bunny* or Bill Martin, Jr.'s and John Archambault's *Chicka Chicka Boom Boom* also feature some of the same appeal. Richard Scarry's classic *The Best Word Book Ever* will appeal to children's desire to increase their vocabularies. Imitating mommy or daddy may also provide good subject matter for children in this range. Any book for this age group should provide an occasion for big, lively, colorful pictures, because young ones will spend most reading time looking at the pictures and identifying by name each thing appearing therein. Here are some types of books that may be appropriate for children in this range:

helping mommy/daddy
I'm like mommy/daddy
new sibling
dressing self
exploring surroundings
word recognition
number recognition

same/different recognition
when I was a baby
my busy day
playground
preschool
transitional object (blanket/baby toy)
new shoes
brushing teeth/dentist visit
all around town
swimming/beach experience

Physical Characteristics

taller

several or all teeth

more hair

increasing muscle definition

Milestones

walking

potty training

talking

first haircut

completion of teething

changing from crib to bed

Physical Activities

toddling

brushing teeth

talking

imitating elders/parents

throwing

feeding self

dropping

undressing/dressing

biting

napping

teething

Clothing

overalls

boots

shoes

slicker

socks

rain hat

underwear (older)

pinafore

snowsuit

suspenders

Objects in Toddler's World

bed (older)
potty (older)
push toys (e.g., popcorn
    popper)
pull toys (e.g., doggy toy)
wading pool
sandbox
merry-go-round
swing
high chair (younger)

tricycle (older)
stroller (younger)
harness
blocks
nesting toys
water wings
toy xylophone
toy box
books
balls

Places in Toddler's World

preschool
play group
store
park
bicycle seat (parent's bike)

dentist's office
barbershop
child's room
grandparents' house

Words for Crying

howling
yowling

sobbing

EARLY CHILDHOOD (THREE YEARS–SIX YEARS)

We now approach the core group of readers for picture books. Children in this range are walking, talking individuals who are becoming more independent of the family environment, developing attachments outside the home and increasing in the sophistication of their comprehension of the world.

At the same time, children of this age have assimilated some of their independence from parents better than they had when they were "terrible" two-year-olds. Children now want to emulate their parents while maintaining some assertiveness. Children move beyond imitation, mimicking mechanical actions, to identification with the parents' more far-reaching activities and modes of behavior—work, dress, mannerisms, etc. Children closely observe and absorb many of their parents' attitudes toward their work, their chores, their mates and others.

The flip side of this emulation is the beginning of clearly defined Oedipal feelings. Many children begin to feel a strong emotional bond with the parent of the opposite sex and unconsciously want that parent all to themselves. There is a concomitant growth of jealous feelings toward the parent of the same sex. Toward the end of this phase, with increased exposure to the outside world, children again grow away from these feelings and begin to model themselves on their peer group. A new school of thought has grown up around the theory that, genetics aside, peer-group influence eclipses the influence of parents. However, peer-group influence begins to be felt only after children have begun spending significant blocks of time in the world outside the home. In today's world, that time may begin for a child as young as three months old, when mommy's maternity leave ends and the child finds herself in day care for most of the day.

Though increasingly able to explore the world for themselves, and to express in words the discoveries they make, young children are still rather restricted in the sphere of their activities. Thus, they reach out to the world with their imaginations. When learning abstract information, they try to place themselves in an imagined scenario that fits the facts. As a complement to this great imaginative development, children may begin to experience fears derived from imagining themselves in different situations. Fears of the dark, of death and of injury may come into play. Children may also become aware of genuine anatomical differences between the sexes. Here are a few topics that stimulate young children's imaginations and may provide material for children's books:

sunset	wind blowing
night sounds	animals
shadows	how things are made
clouds	where things come from
falling leaves	color of the sky
flowers blooming	moon/stars
where babies come from	

Children in this age group ask lots of questions. At the same time, parents have more help than before in answering some questions, for these children have started formal schooling. This engenders inevitable anxiety about separation from the parents, fitting in with peers, etc. This transition has been a rich topic for authors of children's books.

There is a wealth of classic children's books for children in this age group. Maurice Sendak's *Where the Wild Things Are* is a frank exploration of the child's darker imaginings and his ability to master them. Beatrix Potter's *The Tale of Peter Rabbit* satisfies the need for a moral universe while allowing the child to feel he can transgress but be welcomed back into the family fold (Janette Sebring Lowrey's *The Poky Little Puppy* is a somewhat more prosaic exploration of the same theme). Hardie Gramatky's *Little Toot* and Watty Piper's *The Little Engine That Could* give voice to a child's aspirations and ability to achieve. Crockett Johnson's *Harold and the Purple Crayon* is a book that satisfyingly develops the ideas of imagination and exploration.

Newer picture books also touch on universal themes for these readers. Peggy Rathmann's *Officer Buckle and Gloria* uses a dog character to illustrate how a child's natural exuberance can enhance but not replace experience. In *Stellaluna* by Janell Cannon, the bat heroine is able to use her different experiences to make and keep friends. *No, David!* by David Shannon explores a young child's difficult moods, while William Steig's *Pete's a Pizza* shows family togetherness and fun.

It is in this age group that anthropomorphic characters may become most prominent. Children in this range have more developed imaginations than their younger selves and may perhaps be better able to relate to people in animals' clothing. *Where the Wild Things Are* is a superb example of when it is appropriate to use such characters: when embodying the darker elements of a child's psyche, his difficult emotions. The classic fairy tales may also be good choices for children in this group, as those stories subtly express the Oedipal challenge the children themselves are confronting. Bruno Bettelheim's classic *The Uses of Enchantment* illuminates the important role of fairy tales in guiding children through this difficult growth and is must reading for any serious student of children's books. You can play variations on the themes of these great stories by adding a new wrinkle all your own—for instance, by retelling the familiar story from the point of view of the villain (e.g., *The True Story of the Three Little Pigs* by Jon Scieszka).

Books that reinforce the child's early learning—such as alphabets, counting books, books about relational concepts and nature—are wonderful supplements at this age. Children may begin to reflect about when they were babies and may want to imagine taking care of a baby, as well as think about emulating their parents in other ways. As children come increasingly into conflict with other children, simple lessons about conflict resolution through compromise may be valuable.

Milestones

going to school	teeth falling out

Physical Activities

crossing the street	caring for a pet
riding a two-wheeler	telling time
saying bad words	reading
putting things away	drawing
hopping	coloring
running	wetting the bed
climbing	sculpting
drawing	painting
playing house	tying shoes
playing doctor	attending parties
dressing up	trick or treat
early chores	papier-mâché

Things in Child's World

bike helmet	desk
swings	easel
jungle gym	bicycle
tricycle	doll
wagon	clay

training wheels	Big Wheel
kite	jump rope
crayons	stuffed animals
paints	books

Places in Child's World

school	grandma's house
classroom	friend's house
playground	Discovery Zone
school bus	zoo
principal's office	Chuck E. Cheese

LATER CHILDHOOD (SIX YEARS–ELEVEN YEARS)

During this long stretch, children further the work of becoming independent of home and family. Their focus may shift to activities, settings and individuals outside the home: School, teachers and friends loom large. As a result, children's self-involvement decreases during these years, and they are better able to assimilate abstract learning. In other words, they are able to understand facts and concepts without having direct pesonal experience of them. At the same time, a consciousness of the consequences of their own actions is developing, increasing feelings of responsibility and resolution. For example, children may understand that hurtful words or blows cause tears and pain; that lying may lead to trouble; that wanting to master a skill requires self-discipline.

Here are some areas where children may begin to develop greater responsibility:

looking after a younger child/sibling
wanting/caring for a pet
helping others
befriending someone "different"
caring for an impaired parent
community/political involvement
learning/assimilating compromising truth about parent
confronting political/economic/historical crisis

assuming responsibilities of a dead parent
standing by a friend in trouble
telling the truth despite consequences
developing feelings about the opposite sex
confronting a bully
self-evaluation and change

Older children may continue to revere their parents but are apt
to feel less comfortable with overt expressions of affection. Children
have other adult role models against whom to measure their parents,
and may begin to regard the ideas of other adults as equal to or better
than those espoused by parents. Some adult characters who may exert
influence in these children's lives include the following:
teacher
coach
older sibling
older friend/coworker
boyfriend/girlfriend
boss/supervisor
social worker
grandparent or other older relative
community "character" or outcast
survivor of calamity
religious advisor
homeless person
celebrity or role model
"bad" character, e.g., drug dealer, thug

Overall these children are beginning to make up their own minds.
This independence may be expressed in other ways, small acts of rebellion such as not washing before dinner or failing to pick up clothes.
Rebellion can take many forms, some quite dramatic. Here are examples of ways in which older children may act out their difficult feelings:
refusing to go on a family outing
neglecting a chore/responsibility
sneaking out of the house
disregarding a curfew

These children can now walk, talk, learn and do things for themselves. They are more interested in the behavior of their peers than in the models provided by parents. This is the period when children form cliques or feel excluded, when standards for what is "cool" or "not cool" are set and mercilessly maintained. Factors that may weigh in the "cool/not cool" calculus include the following:

clothes	primary group of friends
hairstyle	bicycle
shoes	wealth
slang	social status
sports/hobbies	siblings
tough/brave	school performance

Children may also obtain a stronger sense of how they fit into the scheme of things—whether they are bright, popular, athletic, etc.—by comparing themselves with others or by hearing others' sometimes unkind assessments.

Due to all the outside influences, children in this group may begin to develop a strong sense of their own independent interests in academics, sports, arts or other areas. Moreover, at this stage children have the motor coordination to enjoy and even master aspects of these activities. Girls and boys both discover sports and other physical activities they enjoy. Girls may more often gravitate toward classic "girl" activities, like ballet and horses, boys toward ice hockey and tackle football. However, any activity may be less gender-defined than it was in the past, and writers should not stereotype activities or participants in them. Generally, these children favor games or other recreational activities that have rules and/or require skill to perform properly. During these ages, children begin to enjoy organized groups like Boys Scouts and Girl Scouts that combine learning skills, social contact with other children and fun outings. Activities children may begin to enjoy include the following:

camping	ballet
hiking	tap dancing
baseball	beauty pageants
football	martial arts (karate, judo, tae
soccer	kwon do)

figure skating	singing
ice hockey	playing a musical instrument
basketball	performing
wrestling	drawing

An opportunity for writers exists to communicate more directly with children in this age range because these children are more likely to choose their own reading material without parental intervention. Children with mobility and allowances may buy comic books or other matter favored by their peers. The variety of books for these children is very wide, ranging from more sophisticated picture books, to "easy-to-read" books, to chapter books, to beginning novels. Informational books and stories of heroes and role models may be popular in this age group. Generally children may look for the following qualities in a hero or heroine:

exceptional skill
courage
independence
some juvenile qualities
some rejection of conventional/adult world
overcoming adversity

The *Eyewitness* series of nonfiction books is very good for these readers. For beginning readers, the Dr. Seuss books and the I Can Read series are excellent. *Best Enemies* by Patricia Leverich is an early chapter book that humorously conveys some of the social challenges confronted by schoolchildren. The realistic novels of writers like Beverly Cleary and Jean Little are excellent for children toward the upper end of this age bracket.

Milestones

first sleepover
scholastic or athletic accomplishment
first responsibility (e.g., pet care, baby-sitting)

Physical Characteristics

taller

stronger

permanent teeth

Activities

baseball

tap dancing

skating

gymnastics

in-line skating

horseback riding

basketball

swimming

wrestling

school

football

chores

soccer

shopping

ballet

collecting

Places in Child's World

baseball diamond

church/synagogue

basketball court

Sunday school/Hebrew school

skating rink

swimming pool

soccer field

mall

football field

arcade

classroom

park

library

school

bookstore

Objects in Child's World

comic books

games

bat

puzzles

baseball glove

books

in-line skates

hockey stick

basketball

tennis racquet

baseball

tent

soccer ball

yo-yo

saddle

video games

stamps

football

coins

Clothes

jersey	toe shoes
tutu	leotard
riding habit	knee socks
team uniform	school uniform
cleats	jeans
high-top sneakers	friendship bracelet
tennis shoes	T-shirts
tap shoes	

ADOLESCENCE (TWELVE YEARS AND UP)

The signal event for children in this age group is the onset of puberty, with all it entails. Children begin to mature physically, with dramatic changes in their physical development. For many, emotional development may not keep pace with the physical changes. This situation may produce some tension, as the body of an adult must be managed by an individual with the emotional makeup of a child. Some of this tension may be acted out in more sophisticated forms of rebellion against parental authority.

Adolescents are strongly conditioned to achieve greater independence from their families. This is the age of rebellion, which may be acted out in any of a variety of ways, including the following:

trying cigarettes
experimenting with drugs
exploring sex
outlandish hairstyle/color
grungy clothes
loud/disagreeable music
tattoos
body piercing
flunking classes
wearing makeup
"cutting" school
friendship with disreputable characters
spending time with older/different kids

formulating distinctive religious/political beliefs
organized protest activities
telling family secrets

Another wrinkle is provided by the fact that a child may not keep pace with his friends in his physical/emotional development. The most obvious example of this situation is the common saw that "girls mature faster than boys." The cliché is often true, and a boy who has grown up with a close female friend of his own age may feel abashed at the dramatic changes in her appearance and feelings while he apparently remains a child. However, friends of the same sex may also mature at different rates. A child who matures slowly may be an object of ridicule to others in his peer group. Moreover, rapid or slow development may indicate hormonal imbalances or other physical conditions entailing different sets of emotions.

The need for independence may lead the child to work outside the home for the first time. Jobs for these young adults could include the following:

delivery person	pet sitter
shop clerk	companion to elderly person
stock person	performer
farm helper	tutor
shoeshine person	counselor-in-training
food server	movie usher
baby-sitter	messenger

At the same time, the child's success at school will become more a matter of his own self-motivation to achieve. He is less likely to turn to a parent for help with homework, and in any event is likely to crave a wide zone of privacy that allows him to do things for himself. At the older end of adolescence, a young person is apt to learn to drive and thus achieve a remarkable degree of independence and mobility.

Together with physical maturity come heightened sexual feelings. Pubescent boys and girls may become acutely aware of body image. They may be self-conscious if they feel they are developing faster or slower than peers. The child may also become aware of how the body appears to members of the opposite sex. Adolescents may place extra emphasis on clothes, hair, skin and other aspects of appearance. This is an age where the primary arbiters of taste and appropriate behavior become the peer group and not the parents or other adults.

At the outset of puberty, girls generally mature faster than boys. Thus, if you are writing about children in junior high school, remember that the girls are likely to be taller and more adult in appearance than the boys. By the early high-school years, the boys have pretty much caught up to the girls. At this point, peer dating may become a poignant issue for treatment in fiction. Such books as Judy Blume's *Forever*, *Past Forgiving* by Gloria D. Miklowitz, and Ellen Conford's *Crush: Stories* have explored young-adult dating issues with sensitivity.

Adolescents test the boundaries of their independence. They may protest or rebel against their parents' rules but still crave a fairly stable environment with clear limits. They may act out their rebellion in a variety of ways, many of which can provide fodder for compelling stories.

Adolescents may be ready to read books written and published for adults. However, they can still benefit from well-crafted fiction and nonfiction directed especially at them. Judy Blume is very sensitive to growing young people's feelings about changes in their bodies and attitudes toward the opposite sex. Paula Fox, Robert Cormier, Paul Zindel, Chris Crutcher, Chris Lynch, Rob Thomas, Francesca Lia Block, Rodman Philbrick and many others approach difficult social issues in a dramatic and entertaining way for these oldest readers of books for young people.

Milestones

puberty	driving
dating	

Physical Attributes

breasts	muscle development
acne	strong appetite
facial hair	trendy haircut
body hair	"cool" clothes
growth spurt	

Activities

sleeping	metalworking projects
team sports	auto repair
cheerleading	work
dancing	baby-sitting
playing music	school dances
movies	hanging out at the mall
school plays	playing video games
science projects	talking on the telephone
carpentry projects	

TYPES OF BOOKS IN EACH AGE GROUP

The following is a glossary of the types of books commonly published for children in the different age groups.

Infants and Toddlers (Birth–Age Three)

Bath book: Puffy plastic books printed with waterproof inks and intended to float in the tub.

Board books: Books printed on sturdy cardstock pages; sometimes a board book is die-cut into an interesting shape related to the theme of the story.

Cloth books: Books printed on soft fabric pages, usually only eight or ten pages in length, with very simple artwork.

Shape books: Any book die-cut into an interesting shape, including softcovers.

Touch-and-feel books: Books with different activities and textures placed throughout to give a child an interactive experience of the book's topic.

Young Children (Ages Three–Six Years)

Novelty books: Picture books with special "value-added" features, like pop-ups, puzzle pieces, stickers, etc.

Picture books: Books, usually thirty-two pages in length, that feature artwork on every page and that tell stories through the interaction of art and text.

Older Children (Ages Six–Eleven Years)

Chapter books: Books that are almost entirely text and are divided into short chapters.

Easy-to-read books: Books featuring more text than art, written on topics of high interest to young people and prepared with controlled vocabulary and frequent repetition.

Middle-grade fiction: Short, simple novels for children who are confidently reading on their own.

Adolescents (Ages Twelve and Up)

Young adult (YA) fiction: Full-fledged novels often written specifically about the special challenges faced by contemporary young people. YA fiction can comprise all the genres of adult fiction, including:

romance
mystery
horror
suspense
historical novel
fictionalized biography

Mass-market series are another popular area in YA fiction, as these young readers may get hooked on particular characters or authors and want to continue beyond the first book. Such series may be based on characters first popularized on television or in the movies, like the one using characters from the film *Clueless*. Others may be books on similar themes by the same author, like Matt Christopher's popular sports stories. The series format may satisfy a need for continuity in a time of young people's lives that is fraught with change.

Chapter Two

Ideas

The first great challenge of writing for children is identifying where you get ideas. We always say that writers don't "have" ideas so much as they "recognize" ideas. Ideas are floating in the air around you. Ideas are in your own head, your own experience and the experiences going on around you all the time. Here are some signals to help you recognize when children's book ideas are coming your way:

you say "when I was a child . . ."
another says "when I was a child . . ."
you observe a parent and child interacting
you observe children playing together
you tell an anecdote about your children
another tells an anecdote about his children
you recall a vivid incident from childhood
your child does/says something dramatic/funny
you observe animals
you and your child share a new experience
you recall a "first time" from your own childhood
your child has a special challenge/fear/question

It is easy to get started if you think about the truly universal experiences that virtually all children have. Start with a list of basic childhood experiences:

birthday
holiday preparation
holiday celebration
starting school
visiting the doctor/dentist

new sibling
new home
making friends
losing/finding things
getting a pet
dressing yourself
parting with beloved object (e.g., blankie, stuffed toy)
learning new things (reading, writing, numbers)
visiting the zoo
family outing (beach/park/shopping trip)
vacation
summer camp
learning to ride a bike

For children in the middle grades and adolescents, some of these scenarios will continue to be relevant (e.g., Christmas, birthday, family outing), though the child's feelings will become more complex. In addition, other universal experiences will become pertinent as children grow older:

disagreeing with authority figures
bonding with peers
defining self-image
learning to drive
first boy-girl party
first date
first kiss
making/not making the team
taking responsibility
working for money/goal
experimenting with smoking/drinking/drugs
developing ideals

You need to think about the experience and the special individual touch you can bring to it. Below we list several of these universal experiences together with certain trappings almost always associated with these experiences. These trappings are suggestions only and should in no way limit your imagination. Rather, this list is designed to illustrate how you can expand your thinking and begin to dress the bare bones of your idea in distinctive colors.

COMMON EXPERIENCES FOR YOUNG CHILDREN

Birthday

cake shaped like a cartoon character
balloons in animal shapes
grab bag of toy musical instruments
piñata shaped like a bull
party dress
party hats with paper fringe
candles shaped like dinosaurs
musical instruments
horns
sparklers
party hats
noisemakers
gifts for guests
tiny baskets of candy
candle holder shaped like a railroad train
basement
backyard
pin the tail on the donkey
clown
magician
face painting
singing
pizza
ice cream
streamers

Visit to the Zoo

feeding time	cotton candy
tram	cable car
peanuts	popcorn

lemonade

polar bear

lion

giraffe

trees

turnstile

balloon

monkey house

clock with animal figures

bubble gum on pavement

baby elephants

insect house

petting area

gift shop

Christmas

stockings

Yule log

Christmas balls

tinsel

tree skirt

tree stand

Christmas tree lot

carolers

candy canes

department-store Santa

sidewalk Santa

Salvation Army bell ringer

decorated store windows

stenciled snowflakes on
    windows

electric candles

Christmas lights

electric snowman yard
    decoration

midnight mass

The Nutcracker ballet

Christmas pageant

living creche

television specials

reindeer lawn ornaments

presents

shopping

leaving cookies and milk

Christmas stockings

Day at the Beach/Learning to Swim

seashells

crabs

clams

sand castle

pail

shovel

bathing suit

ice cream

whitecaps

dunes

inflatable ball

sunglasses

sunblock

mermaid's purse

seaweed

sanderlings

seagulls

lifeguard station

sea-monster float

water wings

inflatable ring
raft
buoy
motorboats
Jet Skis
water-skiers
clouds
tide pools
sandbars
shower
beach umbrella

flip-flops
cooler
blanket
towel
footprints
squishy sand
surfboard
solar-powered radio
wet suit
limpets

Picnic

checkered blanket
prickly grass
wicker basket
cooler
shade trees
ants
sunsuit
hide-and-seek
robin
lizard
sun hat
barbecue grill

Thermos
cloth napkins
clover
mud pies
green onions
stray dog
picket fence
rain poncho
wild berries
potato salad
hot dogs

First Day of School

blackboard
teacher's aide
children of different
    races/ethnicities
cubbyhole
nap time
snack time
recess
mat

lunch box
American flag
pledge of allegiance
piano
"America the Beautiful"
letter stencils
bulletin board
apple
milk and cookies

chalk

eraser

world map

globe

aquarium

terrarium

playground

computer terminal

teacher

principal

crayons

paper

books

Elmer's glue

paste

construction paper

new school clothes

Doctor/Dentist Visit

waiting room

magazines

stacking toys

scale

examining table with
   white paper

dentist's chair

tiny mirror for inside
   mouth

pick

reflex mallet

flashlight for ears/mouth

tongue depressor

hypodermic needle

lab coat

injection

examination

stethoscope

X ray

light box

lollipop

new toothbrush

dental drill

eye chart

alcohol wipe

latex gloves

plaster cast

anatomical/dental chart

life-size replica of teeth

cotton swabs

doctor

dentist

nurse

special toothpaste

floss

Play Date

friend's room

swing

dollhouse

chutes and ladders

basement

backyard

woods

climbing tree

exploring

finding buried treasure

hide-and-seek
playing catch
model airplanes
jungle gym
dress up
crayons
toy chest
pup tent
marionette

checkers
erector set
toy trucks
blocks
finger paints
stickers
coloring books
dolls

Moving to a New Home

packing
cartons
moving van
tape
twine
"for sale" sign
garage sale
packing/unpacking
old friends/new friends
moving men (workers)
markers

feeling lonely
exploring
saying good-bye
meeting new people
choosing paint color
helping paint
new curtains
deciding where things go
wallpaper
things left behind

Going to the Store

shopping cart
salesperson
cashier
shelves
display case
tape measure
cash register
security guard
mall
parking lot
stacks of goods

piles of goods
"do not touch"
breaking merchandise
trying things on
leaving room to grow
things you need/don't need
money
escalator
public address system
lost and found

Getting a Pet

choosing a pet
petting
feeding
grooming
playing
cleaning up
exercising
sleeping
naming
bathing
walking
choosing a leash

getting scratched
getting angry
teaching obedience
learning responsibility
paper training
house training
pet bed
pet door
box with shredded newspaper
ticking clock
bottle feeding

New Sibling

pregnant mommy
new baby
naming
crying
feeling neglected
jealousy
holding
feeding
playing
helping pick a name
hospital
other relatives visiting

telling about when I was born
being older/responsible
crib
baby toys
blanket
gifts
bottles
being quiet at baby's nap time
sharing mommy/daddy
acting out
twins/triplets

COMMON EXPERIENCES FOR OLDER CHILDREN

Starting Middle School

changing classrooms
class bells
different teachers
children from different
areas/backgrounds

"cool" clothes
new slang
team sports
different/harder subjects
trendy haircuts

learning foreign languages
brain vs. nerd
special teacher
taking bus/bike to school
gym class

expensive sneakers
firearms/metal detectors
cafeteria lunches
lockers

Dating

first dance
fancy or "cool" dress
makeup
hairdo
confiding in friends
secret crush
anonymous notes
changing appearance/
    manner

practicing kissing
borrowing the car
paying for a date
corsage
heels
group date
holding hands
giving pin/ring/other jewelry
age-rated movies

TRIED-AND-TRUE TOPICS

As we suggested in chapter one, different topics may be more appropriate for different age groups. Children have different developmental challenges and needs at different ages, and the same subject matter may not work equally well for a toddler and an older child. Below we list "tried-and-true" topics by age of the reader.

Infant (Birth–One Year)

bath time
supper time
bedtime
animal sounds
farm animals
Mother Goose

peekaboo
baby's day
finger rhymes
lullabies
shapes
colors

Toddler (One Year–Three Years)

words
teething

potty training
new sibling

exploring the world
playing with others
sleeplessness
mischief
saying no
rhymes
simple folktales
imitating mommy or
daddy
dressing/undressing

tricycle
preschool
play group
store
transitional object (blanket,
old toy)
I'm a big boy/girl
numbers
letters

Early Childhood (Three Years–Six Years)

fear of the dark
first day of school
wild animals
pets
alphabet
counting
when you were a baby
cars and trucks
manners
too little
questions and answers
anthropomorphic
characters
classic fairy tales
books about relational
concepts (relative
sizes; same/
different)
nature

taking care of baby
compromise
parents
teeth falling out
riding a two-wheeler
putting things away
playing house
playing doctor
dress up
early chores
caring for a pet
wetting the bed
tying shoes
playground
school bus
illness
separating from primary
caregiver

Later Childhood (Six Years–Eleven Years)

school
competition
favorite teacher

disliked teachers
friends
people who are different

learning differences
handicaps
best friends
acts of rebellion
cliques
"cool"/"not cool"
academics
sports
arts
ballet
horses
organized groups
learning skills
social contact with other children
fun outings
"easy-to-read" books

first sleepover
tap dancing
gymnastics
horseback riding
swimming
school
chores
shopping
collecting stamps/coins
dinosaurs
astronomy
true stories
biographies
natural disasters
world records
summer camp

Adolescence (Twelve Years and Up)

puberty
emotional development
rebellion
working outside the home
self-motivation
learning to drive
sexual feelings
body image

appearance
peer group
dating
team sports
cheerleading
school plays
school projects

TOPICS THAT CROSS AGE BOUNDARIES

Although different topics may be more frequently developed for certain age groups, a good story on any topic will work if you're able to develop a convincing, age-appropriate point of view for your characters. For instance, stories about new babies in the family are most often seen in picture books for young children whose parents have not yet completed their families. However, a "new baby" story could work well for adolescents. Teen pregnancy is one possibility. Another possibility is a story involving the parents' "change of life" baby who becomes a new sibling to an adolescent already dating and driving. Surely that adolescent's feelings will be complex, valid and interesting, albeit in some ways very different from the feelings he would have had about a new brother when he himself was a small child. Here are a few ideas to try crossing the boundaries between age groups and subject matter:

Infants, Toddlers and Young Children

parent or older sibling starting school
parent going (back) to work
parent or older sibling selecting a mate
driving with parent or older sibling
going to (daddy's) job
developing religious convictions/ideals

Middle-Grade Children and Adolescents

new baby in the family
family outing
holiday celebration
starting school (middle/high/boarding)
illness (e.g., sports injury)
making (different) friends
when you were younger (body changes)

DIFFICULT TOPICS

Of course, as described in the introductory material of chapter one, the experiences described apply mostly to the average child or family. However, many books for all ages confront less usual issues, "problems" confronted by some but not all or even most families. Such books can provide support for children who find themselves in difficult situations, or can provide the more fortunate reader with a dramatic story that increases his compassion for others and appreciation of his own situation. The following topics can be handled different ways for different readers. For instance, a sensitive story about parents' divorce might feature anthropomorphic animals for the younger reader, as a means of adding a comfort zone of fantasy to the painful subject matter. For older children, human characters would certainly be the protagonists of choice. A book about homosexuality for younger children might take the form of a story like Johnny Valentine's *One Dad, Two Dads, Brown Dad, Blue Dads*, where the child discovers a comfort level with his homosexual father and the father's partner. A very different approach would apply in a story about an adolescent confronting his own budding homosexual feelings, for instance, *Good Moon Rising* by Nancy Garden.

Social Challenges

moving away
going to a new school
making/losing friends
dealing with a bully
being/feeling different
confronting prejudice
racism
sexism
anti-Semitism
liking/disliking the opposite sex
overcoming shyness
rejection from team/play/"in" group
rejection due to economic class
peer pressure
alcohol/drugs

Family Challenges

parents' divorce
adoption
abandonment
neglect
death of parent/sibling/
   grandparent

physical abuse of parent
physical abuse of child
parent's use of guns
parent's use of drugs/alcohol
parent's unemployment
teenage pregnancy

parent's homosexuality	molestation
child's homosexuality	blended families
incest	stepparents and stepsiblings

Geopolitical Challenges

deposed royalty	crop failure
ethnic cleansing	conquest
nuclear fallout	exile
economic collapse	genocide
ecological disaster	nomadic lifestyle
famine	gangs/gang wars
siege	inner-city life

Physical/Mental Challenges

cystic fibrosis	teenage pregnancy
muscular dystrophy	hemophilia
cerebral palsy	autism
epilepsy	Down's syndrome
leukemia	chemical dependency
disability	psychosis
dyslexia	obsessive-compulsive disorder
attention deficit with	bipolar disorder
hyperactivity	schizophrenia
disorder	

Climatic/Geographic Challenges

volcano	flood
hurricane	tropical storm
tornado	isolation
tsunami	drought
typhoon	avalanche

EDUCATIONAL TOPICS

In addition to books that give emotional support, children need books to reinforce the concepts they learn in school. From the very earliest ages, children's books can cover topics for learning. Throughout the picture-book ages, authors can seize opportunities to include or reinforce information about these topics even in stories not meant to teach; by mentioning the numbers of things in a picture, the colors or shapes of objects shown, or helping children remember things they've already learned. From the early rhyme of "Rub-a-dub, dub," which conveys something about the number three, to Tana Hoban's photographic essays on shape, color and contrast, to Ruth Heller's inventive books about parts of speech, there are innumerable entertaining ways to convey educational concepts to children. But remember to consult this list even if you are writing a story that is "just for fun," so you can look for places to reinforce something children need to learn.

Learning Concepts

alphabet	manners
numbers	nature
colors	cause and effect
shapes	geography
sizes	weather
sounds	stars and planets
opposites	human body
word recognition	animals
telling time	plants
safety	

INCLUDE DESCRIPTION

For older children, beyond the picture-book range, verbal description is very important. Detailed descriptions of the physical reality help readers make the transition to text-only books by letting them visualize exactly what's happening without the crutch of pictures. In this way, young readers begin to draw meaning from the words themselves and see that a significant reality may be conveyed by the written word. Thus, you build learning into your writing not by including specific concepts where appropriate but by illustrating what reading is all about. Here are some factors to describe in detail in books for older children:

Physical Appearance

hair color/style/length/texture
eye color/size/shape
skin color/texture
relative height
relative weight
other features (nose, ears, lips, teeth, limbs, etc.)

Decor

furniture	ceiling
paint	windows
wallpaper	doors
floor	comfort

Clothing

color	warmth
texture	closure
fabric	style
weight	

Food

taste	quantity
color	appearance
smell	strange/familiar
temperature	

Sounds

voices	volume
music	pleasant/unpleasant
sirens	tonality (shrill/mellow)
birds	resonance (echoing/swelling/
house noises	diminishing)

NONFICTION TOPICS

Rather than weaving factual material or nature-based descriptions into your book, you may prefer to write nonfiction for young people. Nonfiction can cover a wide range of topics, and any topic can be treated in more or less detail for different age groups. Many so-called experts have said that nonfiction is less enriching or inspiring than fiction for young readers. Anyone making such a statement can never have read the nature writing of Joanne Ryder, the biographies by Ingri and Edgar Parin d'Aulaire or the social histories of Milton Meltzer. Nonfiction writing can be as imaginative and enriching as fiction, even more so if it is approached in an inventive and open spirit and touches on a topic truly dear to the writer.

Some of the best topics are the following:

Animals

cats	elephants
dogs	giraffes
horses	prairie dogs
cows	coyotes
pigs	buffalo
goats	praying mantis
chickens	bees
ducks	ants
geese	spiders
sheep	sharks
lions	whales
tigers	pet care
bears	

Prehistory

tyrannosaurus	cave dwelling
apatosaurus	cave paintings
Cro-Magnon Man	Neanderthals
Australopithecus	woolly mammoths
pterosaurs	saber-toothed tigers

magnolia trees

big bang

origins of life

Astronomy and Earth Science

solar systems

other worlds

Hubbell space telescope

Apollo missions

Mariner

gas giants

Sea of Tranquility

sunspots

meteor showers

Halley's comet

Copernicus

gravity

Mir

Ursa Major/Minor

Orion the Hunter

zodiac

Coriolis force

cyclones/anticyclones

plate tectonics

Pangaea

ozone layer

recycling

Human Body

skeleton

where babies come from

puberty

teeth

circulation

elimination of waste

digestion

enzymes

germs/bacteria

zygotes

chromosomes

cell division

growth

muscle development

exercise/fitness

nutrition

preventive health care

becoming a doctor/nurse/
    technician

first aid

menstruation

History

Children's Crusade

Battle of the Bulge

D-day

Battle of Bull Run/Battle
    of Manassas

Boston Tea Party

Minutemen

Fort Sumter

Battle of New Orleans

suffragism

Emancipation	Auschwitz
Proclamation	Cultural Revolution
Spanish Armada	Berlin Wall
voyages of discovery	Bosnia
conquest of Gaul	
land of the Pharaohs	

You may be concerned that any topic for a children's book has been written about many times before, and you may wonder what you can bring to the topic that is new. Of course, you bring you own special sensibility and enthusiasm for the idea. But often the best, most original ideas come from slapping together two tried-and-true ideas: dinosaur alphabet, counting cats, colors of the planets, etc. Below is a mix-and-match list of ideas for different age categories:

Experience	Concept
visit with grandparents	manners
trip to the beach	stars and planets
first day of school	counting
imaginative play	alphabet
new sibling	dinosaurs
Christmas	colors
new home	shapes
visit to farm or zoo	sounds

It may seem daunting that many excellent books already exist on so many of these topics. You may also be concerned that many of these topics are covered in textbooks and other educational materials children receive at school. Your challenge is to make your chosen idea fresh. Children will turn to your nonfiction book for supplementary information or a different perspective on a topic of great interest. You can help satisfy that need by looking at your topic with one of the following techniques.

Different Point of View

    animal's own perspective
    animal's perspective on another animal

deep-sea diver
space traveler
first-person historical personage
young person acquainted with historical personage
time traveler
scientist
first-person description of life in a different culture
humorist
explorer

Different Emphasis

unexpected size relationships
comparisons
humor
historical time line (evolution of concept or phenomenon)
biography (of zoological, geological or meteorological entity or
    system)
travel narrative (relating geographic concepts)
diary or journal
poetry
lexicon of terms important to subject (dictionary/glossary)
cumulative plot
fictionalized approach (e.g., to biography, history)
combination of fact-inspired narrative with factual sidebars

You may use some or all of these different approaches in creating
your nonfiction book. However, fiction can also be a powerful medium for conveying factual information. A hybrid approach combining fiction and nonfiction has resulted in classics like Esther Forbes's
Johnny Tremain, which combines a compelling novel about a young
boy's growing up with factual information about the beginnings of
the American Revolution. Another approach is typified by the car-
toons featuring Sherman and Mr. Peabody on the *Rocky and Bullwinkle*
television program: In episodes involving humorous time travel, a
boy and his dog effectively teach children that Schubert left an Unfin-
ished Symphony, that there are mysteries surrounding the attribution

of Shakespeare's works, and other facts that might seem sophisticated for a young, cartoon-watching audience. The *Wishbone* television program similarly combines a dog, time travel and accurate information about other times and places. You may be able to develop some interesting techniques through extensive reading and selective viewing.

Other high-interest nonfiction categories include biography, nature topics, sports, religion, skill-building (e.g., drawing, manners, occupations), exotic places, explanations of how things work, explorations of different lifestyles and transportation technology (cars, trucks, boats, planes, etc.).

Remember that children's books are a continuum reflecting children's different skills and needs at different ages. For a toddler, a book about cats might be story about a small kitten and its adventures exploring its world. Such a story would both convey a few things about cats and reflect the child's own sense of being small and learning about a big new world. By letting the small child relate to the kitten, you may also convey the important information that the child should have compassion for the kitten and play nicely with kittens and other small animals when he encounters them.

This sense of sympathy may translate, for the somewhat older child, into a wish to care for a kitten or cat. Now an informational book about cats would be useful, telling some important things about cat anatomy and habits, as well as advice on the feeding and care of cats.

Still later, an in-depth exploration of cat evolution and anatomy may be of exceptional interest to young adults who love animals, are considering a zoology course or preparing for careers in veterinary medicine. We cannot tell you what age group you want to write for but can remind you that any list of book topics for young people is flexible—any subject can be made more or less complex to suit the age and interests of your ideal reader.

A WORD ABOUT THEME

Idea, subject matter and theme may seem like synonyms but they are not. As we have discussed in this chapter, subject matter is the raw material you will turn into a book, like the straw the miller's daughter spun into straw in the fairy tale "Rumpelstiltskin." Your idea is the

way you spin the raw material into the something new and precious—
the unique approach you take to subject matter that may be well
known in its more familiar forms. Theme is the glue that holds your
book together; it is what your book is really *about*.

Joanne Ryder's book *Chipmunk Song* is a picture book in which
an imaginative child puts himself into the world of the chipmunk.
The subject matter is the life and environment of the chipmunk. The
idea is illustrating the facts through a child's-eye perspective. The
theme is the importance of imagination in developing empathy and
respect for nature. The theme is the intention behind the book, its
higher purpose. Every good book has a strong theme, and here is a
list of some of the most basic:

being yourself
growing up
developing positive family relationships
developing positive connections outside the family
increasing independence
sharing
helping others
growing and learning
understanding the environment
understanding God
home
trying new things
telling the truth
taking responsibility
good health/hygiene
establishing positive behavior patterns (e.g., manners)

The concept of theme is somewhat elusive and has elicited many
questions in the workshops and classes we have conducted. Participants have challenged us to identify themes in such "just for fun"
books as Kay Thompson's *Eloise* and H.A. Rey's *Curious George*. Both
books clearly deal with the child's need to play, even when he is
in an environment where play would seem to be inappropriate or
discouraged. Through following their imaginations and instincts, Eloise and George enrich their environments and experiences and have

the childhoods (symbolically, in George's case) that they need in order to grow into creative and self-sufficient individuals.

Unlike your idea, your theme is universal in the sense that the same themes pervade books for children of all ages. The book in which a toddler joins others in the sandbox has the same themes as the book in which an eighth-grader attends her first dance: behaving appropriately with others and maintaining a sense of individual identity. Obviously this theme is elaborated very differently in the two cases. The following list contains examples of how emphasis may be shifted to make the same basic theme work for different age groups.

THEMES BY AGE GROUP

Infant

> self-recognition
> recognition of others
> recognizing patterns
> experiencing new sensations

Toddler

> reinforcement of new skills (e.g., walking, vocabulary
>   development)
> early learning concepts (letters, numbers, colors, shapes)
> comparative concepts (same/different, sizes)
> meeting others
> feeling too small
> growing up
> taking care of self (toilet training/dressing/washing)
> when you were a baby
> outside the home
> separating from parents

Early Childhood

> starting school
> getting along

compromise
encountering new people
encountering new situations
self-discipline (e.g., manners, learning)
learning progress (e.g., word recognition, counting)
introduction to religion
increasing independence

Older Children

being yourself
the world around you
learning about others
cooperation
taking responsibility (e.g., pet, chores)
increasing complexity in learning (e.g., science, reading)
developing ideas (e.g., religion, values)
changing environments/situations (e.g., new home,
middle school)
identifying with peer group

Adolescents

experimentation
rebellion
developing values/politics
questioning authority
establishing new relationships (e.g., sexual)
growing/changing body
increasing independence
increased responsibility
establishing identity

As you can see from the previous lists, there is a consistency in the themes from one age category to another, but at each level a particular theme may be taken to the next step. So, for instance, an infant's body may develop to the point of her being able to focus her gaze on a page and see patterns, or her tactile apparatus may allow her to feel textures. Following the theme of physical development, as a toddler, the same child may be proud that she can walk and has developed the motor skills to fasten simple buttons or snaps. As a young child, her greater strength lets her ride a tricycle, then a bicycle and as an older child she can ride to school. As an adolescent, she will try to master the latest dance steps for the prom. So the theme of physical growth may be a component in all age categories, and its expression will grow with the age of the reader.

Chapter Three

Age Groups and Formats

Books that glow in the dark! Books that sing! Books you can wear! Books that tell stories! Of course, more books fall into the last category than into the others. But there are children's books that do all those other things as well—and more! Books today can appeal to all the five senses. Beautiful books have always appealed to the sense of sight. But now books appeal to the sense of sound with buttons you can push to play music or activate the characters' voices. The sense of touch is indulged in books that let the reader feel different textures of important props or scenic elements in the story. And you can smell all the wonderful odors of a nature walk in a book with fragrance labels affixed at key places in the illustrations. Only the sense of taste goes begging, but surely it is only a matter of time before books will be printed on tasty edible material!

Knowledge of the formats available to you as a children's book writer can be important to your success. Choosing a special format that you know is workable can set your book apart from the rest. But keep in mind the important correlation between the format of your book—its size, length, look and special features—and the story you are telling. In other words, a clever format idea is not enough—it must be part of a satisfying whole.

Even if you do not intend to write a book with a novelty feature, format must be part of your thinking. You should be able to picture the finished book in your mind's eye. Format includes the look, size and shape of your book, the page count, the number and type of illustrations.

If you have never published before, a novelty format may seem a little beyond your reach. Novelty books are often expensive to produce and risky in terms of sales. Nevertheless, writers are well advised to be aware of the myriad possibilities for children's book formats. Thinking of special features will help keep you alive to your book's possibilities—the novelty in a picture book is often the story's most dramatic feature re-created as a pop-up, a sound or a toy. Picturing your story's key element in one of these forms may help you give it the emphasis it needs in your writing or may even help you appreciate and craft the single most important element of your book.

If you have a clever format idea, don't say no to it just because you are not an established author. It may be just the marketing hook your book needs to grab a publisher's attention. Submitting a novelty idea may present some special challenges—you have to think about how the book would be produced and packaged. If your idea is to have a stuffed toy accompany your book, a handmade toy should accompany your book dummy. If your idea involves pop-ups or paper engineering of any kind, you really need a professional to prepare some dummy pages to show your idea will work. Use your judgment; if the special feature is something you can manufacture at home, make it yourself. If not, find a professional to help you. But if the special feature is integral to your proposal, always include a prototype to show off your idea to best advantage. Remember, someone had to come up with *Pat the Bunny* the first time. The book must have looked expensive and difficult to produce back in 1941. But the idea was so compelling that the publisher grabbed it, and publishing history was made.

When deciding to submit a novelty book, research publishers' catalogs before submitting your proposal. Although most of the major children's book publishers now publish some novelty books, there are still some smaller or more old-fashioned houses that resist new format ideas. The reason may be a lack of resources or a sales emphasis on the library market (traditionally, novelty books have been considered too fragile to circulate and too difficult to shelve). If you are sending out a novelty book, make sure you send it to a publisher that welcomes special formats.

In the earlier chapters, we described a few things about young readers of different ages and the different types of books appropriate for each group. In this chapter we will explore the correlation between age and book format in greater depth. The format, like the subject matter, should be age-appropriate. It is a great boon to creators of children's books that they can choose from a wide variety of formats; these choices are not available to writers for adult readers. Yet the fact that older readers are less tolerant of novelties in book formats is something of a paradox: After all, older readers are used to the same black print on white pages and might be expected to seek more stimulating options. Why is it that as readers grow older, they become less tolerant of novelty in books?

This question goes to the heart of why novelty books exist. Novelties exist to invite and entice young readers to pick up books by appending fun and toylike features. The nature of the feature is limited only by the creator's imagination and the manufacturing capabilities of modern book production facilities. However, the feature should also reinforce the act of reading—that is, there should be a thematic link between the subject matter of the book and the novel feature. Ideally, the novelty helps the reader have a tangible, palpable experience of something important in the book, communicating that books convey a type of reality. Presumably, young adults and adult readers already know that books convey reality and so no longer need the special inducements or reinforcement of novelty formats. (See, however, *Griffin and Sabine* by Nick Bantock, which is a novelty book for adults incorporating facsimile correspondence between the protagonists.)

All books must be printed and bound. However, the multitude of available options means that manufacturing is a much more sensitive part of the publishing process for children's books than for most adult books. If you are thinking about writing or illustrating a book with a distinctive format, some of the manufacturing concerns should be part of your thinking. Ask yourself, "Can this be done?" Probably it can; but cost is a key element. And be aware that the more special features you build into your project, the higher the cost of publishing will be. You can be sure that cost will be part of the publisher's concern in considering your book. Familiarity with the vast array of children's book formats will free your creativity; it will also allow you to be realistic and think of options when a cost-sensitive publisher wants to find a cheaper way to publish.

Before exploring different novelties, however, here is a brief glossary of book production terms. A review of these terms will help the writer or illustrator be conversant with the special manufacturing options and challenges that face children's book writers and publishers.

Binding: This is the manner in which the pages of the book are held together inside the covers. There are many different binding options for children's books. Many children's storybooks are *case-bound,* which means the signatures (sets of folded and gathered pages; see definition on p. 63) are sewn together (side-sewn) and glued between board covers. Some books, both hardcover and softcover, are *spiral-bound;* holes are punched near the spine and a plastic or metal comb is inserted to hold the pages together (*Pat the Bunny* has this type of binding). Paperback picture books are often *saddle stitched,* which means the pages are folded and gathered and bound into the cover using heavy-duty metal staples. Longer softcover books (and some hardcover books) are *perfect-bound,* meaning the pages are glued (rather than sewn) together, then glued flush with the spine of the book. There are many other styles of binding, but these are some of the principal ones.

Bleed: Bleed is the extent to which the artwork approaches the edge of the page. "Full bleed" means that the artwork goes all the way to the outer edges of the page. Generally, the artist must create a picture somewhat bigger than the page size in order to have the artwork bleed off the page. Artwork that "bleeds" is desirable because it creates an impression of space and helps the artist keep important pictorial elements centered on the page. It also allows the printer a margin of error in trimming the pages without cutting off important pictorial elements.

Board book: Board books are books printed on thick board pages that are difficult for children to bend or destroy. Because of the thickness of the pages, board books often contain no more than one signature of sixteen pages. These are usually books for very young readers. Here are some additional features that may make board books extra fun for little ones:

rounded corners
die-cut shapes
doors and windows die-cut into pages

Die-cut: During the manufacturing process, the book is mechanically cut into a shape. The entire book may be cut into the shape, or pages may be separately die-cut, providing windows, doors and other elements that allow children to peek, open and guess. There may be progressive die-cuts that slowly reveal an important element about the book. For instance, the Grosset & Dunlap Poke and Look Books have die-cut circles that grow progressively smaller. However, a die-cut can be as simple as a hole cut all the way through your book. Some story elements seem to lend themselves naturally to die-cut shapes. If your story is simple and very focused on one element that is visually strong, think about proposing or designing a die-cut book. Here are a few such elements:

butterfly	house
fish	store
monkey	fire engine
flower	truck
teapot	tricycle
chef's hat	castle

Endpapers: Most books in hardcover bindings have endpapers. These are "extra" pages needed to glue the book together. In a thirty-two-page picture book with "full ends," the book has eight extra pages. That means there are really forty pages in the book, and the endpapers are not counted in calculating the thirty-two pages. The book begins with a half-title page on page 1. In a thirty-two-page picture book with "self-ends," there are really only thirty-two pages in the book. The first four pages may be endpapers, with page 1 pasted down, pages 2-3 decorated and page 4 facing the title page. Some or all of the last four pages would also be endpapers. As you can see, there are fewer story pages in a book with "self-ends."

Fifth color: The combination of the four basic colors—black, yellow, red and blue—can make virtually any color. The addition of a fifth color, usually in a metallic or other unusual ink, can make a dramatic impact in your book.

Folios: Also known as page numbers. Most picture books do not have numbered pages. However, books for the school and library market often do. Any book that requires a table of contents or index must have page numbers.

Front matter: The first few pages of any book are taken up with such information as title, author and artist credits, publisher's name and trademarks, copyright notice, dedication, etc. Where applicable, there may also be a table of contents and other information. All this material is known as *front matter.* Between one and four pages are given over to these preliminaries in most picture books.

Full color: Most picture books today are printed in "full color," also known as four-color process. This printing process allows the printer to re-create the illustrator's palette by using subtle gradations of four cardinal colors: red, yellow, blue and black. The colors are separated into four "plates" (in the days of lithography, these really were printing plates; today they are photographic impressions), and the pages pass through the press four times to take the impression of each color of ink.

Gutter: The gutter is the indentation between two pages of a book. The gutter has special significance in children's books, which are mostly illustrated. The pictures should be designed so that important elements are kept away from the gutter, as it can be difficult to control exactly how much of each page will fall into the gutter during binding.

Jacket: Many hardcover picture books are published with jackets, decorated wrappers printed on heavy coated paper reproducing the title and some important pictorial image from the book. The jacket is a not a universal feature of children's books and usually indicates a high-priced, prestige item.

Lamination: The covers of children's picture books are often laminated to give them a shiny, bright appearance. Other types of coating, such as varnish, are less costly and give the book a duller finish. However, the coating also serves the practical purpose of protecting the book, making the cover more durable and easier to keep clean.

Page count: The page count is an important feature of the book that varies by the format and age of the reader. Most books are printed in multiples of sixteen pages; however, due to their brevity, children's books are sometimes printed in multiples of eight pages. Sixteen is usually the minimum number of pages in a book (cloth books and books printed on vinyl don't have the same constraints as books printed on paper); twenty-four and thirty-two pages are the most common page counts for picture books. As children grow older, books grow longer but are always printed in multiples of sixteen pages.

Paper stock: Because picture books are often illustrated in full color, they must be printed on paper of good weight and opacity. Paper that is too light or porous may absorb the ink or otherwise render the images indistinct. Paper in picture books is often coated (you can feel the smoothness and see the sheen on coated paper) to make the pages more opaque and to give the colors greater brilliance.

Signature: A signature is the group of book pages made from one sheet of paper coming off the printing press. Most often, a press sheet is folded into sixteen pages. The sheet is then folded and cut so the pages appear in their proper order.

Spine: The spine is the flip side of the gutter and is literally the backbone of the book. The spine is a key part of marketing a book, as most books get "spine out" display in bookstores and libraries. The author's name, the title and the publisher's trademarks often appear on the spine. Softcover picture books and some other types of very thin books have no true spines and require special display and marketing techniques to gain recognition in bookstores.

Trim size: The trim size of the book is its square dimensions— width by length. The book is not measured from top-to-bottom and side-to-side of the cover. Rather, the trim size is the size of the pages inside the book, which are almost always somewhat smaller than the cover.

Type: The typeface and size are very important in children's books, as the look of the letters must harmonize with the artwork but must also be big enough and bold enough to be readable. Different, fancier typefaces may be used on the cover and title page of a book. This type is called *display type.*

NOVELTY BOOKS FOR VERY YOUNG CHILDREN

When children are very small, they must be read to. Many novelties may be inappropriate for the very youngest children, as these children do not have the motor coordination to have hands-on experiences with books. Moreover, books featuring small, movable parts are inappropriate as these may present safety hazards to very young children who put things in their mouths, teething children and toddlers who bite, chew and even swallow nonfood items. Novelties among books for the youngest children generally relate to moments in such children's routines—times of day and places where these children often go. Thus, books may be printed on soft cloth pages that can be taken into the carriage or crib and later laundered, puffy plastic pages that won't get soaked in the bath, or chunky board pages that stand up to throwing, chewing and twisting. "Touch-and-feel" books, like *Pet the Baby Farm Animals*, illustrated by Lucinda McQueen, may also work for these little ones if the books do not feature dangerous small pieces that may become dislodged and swallowed, or sharp corners that poke children's eyes.

Here are some formats and features for novelty books for the very young:

Bathtub books: Bathtub books are often printed on vinyl pages that are filled with foam. The materials help the books float in the tub and drip dry when bathtime is over.

Chunky books: Here the word "chunky" is used as a generic descriptive term for little square board books that look almost like building blocks. A number of publishers have books in this format, and such books are fun objects to hold and fondle.

Cloth books: Books are printed on cloth pages. Some books printed on cloth have stuffing or are printed on a type of fabric that makes them suitable for other uses. For instance, a puffy cloth book is like a pillow and could go into the crib. A book printed on terry cloth is like a washcloth and could go into the tub. A subcategory of cloth books features a cloth doll on string that can be manipulated through the pages, placed in pockets, etc., as part of the story.

Flap books: The pages contain paper flaps that can be lifted to reveal surprise scenic elements. Eric Hill's *Where's Spot?* is the perfect example of this type of book. A subcategory is the *gatefold* book. A gatefold is different from a flap glued to the page. It is, rather, an extra length of paper that is folded over to hide part of the scene.

Touch-and-feel books: The preeminent example of this type of book is Dorothy Kunhardt's *Pat the Bunny.* The little book has a different feature on each page: flaps to lift, fragrances to sniff, textures to touch. Some books in this category have only textures on each page, or only fragrances, but the idea is to make a truly interactive book for the smallest children. Here are some special features to build into touch-and-feel books:

> wheel to spin
> scratch-and-sniff labels
> die-cut shapes
> textures to touch
>> "fur"
>> fabric
>> wood
>> sandpaper
>> fuzzy pages
> squeaker
> mirror

A baby book can also be packaged with a special age-appropriate item to make an endearing baby gift. A bathtub book might go well with a bath sponge, while a night-light, key-ring toy or musical lullaby toy might make a good companion to a bedtime book. Think about ways to make the add-on an integral part of the book. One enterprising author had the clever idea of combining a board book with a key-ring toy: Instead of a traditional binding, each board page had a hole punched through one corner and all were attached by a plastic key ring of the kind that babies enjoy. This is the type of idea that can be developed only by a creative author with a knowledge of the audience and of what works with children. Suggest any ideas you have for creative formats to publishers—that's the only way for publishers to get new ideas and for children to get new, creative kinds of books.

NOVELTY BOOKS FOR TODDLERS

In the next age group, children begin to experience the true picture books. These books may also have novelty features, especially for the younger children in this set. However, the novelties can be somewhat more sophisticated, employ more small and moving parts, and help convey motor skills along with the sheer fun of reading and playing. Although you might think otherwise, books featuring pop-ups and moving illustrations are for children a little older—children who have stopped putting books into their mouths, for instance. Pop-ups, pull tabs and like devices are collectively called paper engineering, and they are surprisingly fragile. Children must have the muscular ability to push and pull but not too hard, and must be old enough to have respect for the book as an integral object.

It's very important for you to have a glossary of the terms most commonly used in describing picture books with novelty features. This way, you can sound conversant with the important terms in presenting your book to publishers or in entertaining their ideas for your book. Publishers are very open to novelty ideas from new authors. However, the more you can back up your idea with appropriate professional descriptions, the more credible you will sound when presenting your concept.

Changing picture: Behind the picture is a wheel, which is turned by means of a tab. Another picture replaces the one printed on the page at the turn of the wheel.

Gatefold: Each page is a little longer than the trim of the book, and the extra length folds over to hide a surprise element.

Lift the flap: Each page has a little flap glued onto the page under which hides a surprise element.

Pop-up: As each page is opened, paper engineering causes important and dramatic scenic elements from the text to arise into a three-dimensional display.

Pull the tab: The pages feature paper engineering ''behind the pages.'' The child pulls tabs to see elements of the scenes move and change position.

Scratch and sniff: Fragrance labels are glued onto the pages of the book, allowing children to smell important elements of the story.

Tab books: Books with tabs at the side allow the reader to flip immediately to the most interesting part of the book for him.

Keep in mind that the special format should be thematically related to the content of the book. Say you had an idea for a scratch-and-sniff book about dinosaurs. From the cost point of view, this could be an attractive notion: Since nobody knows what dinosaurs smelled like, the printer could use any leftover fragrance labels at the printing plant and thus save money. However, the fact that smell and dinosaurs are not linked ideas in readers' minds shows that this idea is not necessarily workable editorially. A walk in the woods, a story about getting ready for Christmas or a book of flowers may be better candidates for books using fragrances.

You also want your special feature to increase the reader's interest in your subject matter. Many years ago, there was a series of nonfiction books that included a sheet of large postage-type stamps to be moistened and affixed in designated spaces in the books. Children loved the colorful stamps and loved moistening them and sticking them into the books. But children were less interested in reading the text on the black-and-white pages and were quite uninterested in revisiting the books after the stamps were all in place.

Here is a mix-and-match list of high-interest topics and popular novelties for picture-book readers. See how many interesting combinations you can make.

dinosaurs	glow-in-the-dark ink
human body	textures to touch
cars and trucks	wheels
stars and planets	fragrance labels
weather	stickers
Christmas	music chips
animals	pop-ups

NOVELTY BOOKS FOR OLDER CHILDREN

As the author and/or illustrator moves into books for older children, it is also important to think about the complexity of the artwork. Although a book like Martin Handford's *Where's Waldo?* is a picture book, it is certainly for children at the more sophisticated end of the spectrum. Infants and toddlers relate better to bold, simple images because their eyes and brains are not yet adept at processing complex information. Complicated artwork like that found in *Where's Waldo?* is for children able to make sense of busy visuals.

If you are an illustrator, you must also consider the technique you use and its potential for reproduction. For instance, colored pencil can look grainy when it is printed, whereas acrylic can become dark and muddy. Some professional dyes contain reflective elements and cannot be photographed for color separation. Most picture-book illustrators use watercolor and gouache, as these media allow for brilliant color and enough transparency to ensure clear reproduction. However, collage, tempera, photography and pastels are also successful techniques for illustrating children's books. There are different formats for presenting the artwork within the book, and it may help you think visually to imagine your pages treated in these different ways:

Single page: Most of the time, a page in a picture book contains a picture with text relating to the picture. The single page is the basic building block of your book, advancing the plot while supporting an appealing visual image.

Spread: The most exciting and climactic parts of your story invite treatment as spreads. A spread contains one large picture splashed across two pages, with text accompanying the picture. Spreads should be used to punctuate and highlight the most dramatic moments in the book.

Vignettes: Vignettes are also called "spots." These are small pictures that can be used to show several actions in rapid succession on a single page or spread. Usually each vignette is surrounded by white space to set it off from the others on the same page or spread.

Editorial content obviously varies by age group. For instance, a joke book for infants and toddlers doesn't work because those children are not adept with language and don't have a wide enough frame of reference to "get" the jokes. However, children reading for themselves may respond. Mother Goose, on the other hand, may defy comprehension but satisfies the very youngest child through rhythm, rhyme and the sheer sound of the words. The younger the child, the more patterning in the text may help the child process the content.

But you don't have to write in verse! Study the works of Margaret Wise Brown and Ruth Krauss for good models of ear-catching prose.

Just as you think about the pictures on the page, you can think about the placement of the type. Usually the artist leaves a blank space for the type on each page of a picture book. However, the type can also be placed in a little box or frame within the larger composition of the artwork, or it can run in a light-colored portion of the picture—say, in a blue sky or white cloud. Although matters of design may not seem crucial to the writer's challenge, we believe the prospective author or illustrator must learn to see the picture book as a whole entity—to "think visually." Picturing each page in your book is, we think, crucial to your ability to craft text of just the right length and content.

NOVELTY BOOK PACKAGES

Nowadays, many publishers package their most popular picture books with special extras, such as dolls or audiotapes, without much regard for the age of the intended readers. This "book and . . ." packaging helps the publisher create a new retail life for a best-selling book and gives consumers a nice prepackaged gift. The children's writer should be aware that publishers are loath to invest in such "value-added" features unless and until the book has proven itself to be a strong seller with a character or feature that children particularly love.

On the other hand, some book concepts stand or fall by the addition of a "value-added" item. Workman Publishing has done a very successful series of nonfiction books packaged with items that help the children relate to the subject matter—for instance, a plastic collecting bottle with a book about bugs, or a plastic birdhouse with a book about birds. In these cases, the added item is integral to the subject matter and approach of the book. Klutz Publishing has done a series of "how-to" books on arts-and-crafts topics, and here again, the packaged-in item (modeling clay, paint set) is key to the child's interaction with the book. In most cases, however, any added feature you propose should be able to form part of the actual book. In other words, your proposal for a novelty book about cars and trucks should envision a die-cut book with wheels, rather than a regular hardcover book packaged with a toy truck. For a first-time author, a publisher is more likely to entertain the stand-alone book idea than the "book and . . ." package.

That does not mean you should swallow your idea about packaging a special item with your book if the item is really important to your concept. An author once submitted a proposal for a "book and blankie" package. What a great, inviting idea! And the blanket really added to the story. However, the author had not thought hard enough about how to package the blanket with the book. In the dummy, the banket was stored in a pocket inside the cover. But how would the consumer know it was there? Definitely consider presenting your "book and . . ." idea, if appropriate. But do all the conceptual work necessary in terms of thinking about presentation.

Another aspect that should be top-of-mind for the aspiring author is how the novelty feature is made known to the consumer. Generally, it is important the special feature be evident from the front cover without adding too much extra type. Ideally, the feature can be part of the title: "Glow-in-the-Dark Sun, Moon and Stars," or "The Mummy Jigsaw Puzzle Book." Otherwise, the feature that sets your book apart may get lost in a store's picture-book display.

Here are some added features that can be affixed to the cover or bound inside your book and that may work for picture-book readers:

temporary "tattoos"	pull tabs
jewelry	3-D glasses
jigsaw puzzle pieces	googly eyes
wheels	Band-aids
laces to tie	clock face with movable hands
pop-ups	furry character face

Here are some items that can work with thematically related picture books but should probably be packaged alongside, rather than inside, the book:

rocks and gems	Scotch tape
magnifying glass	spoons
seashells	dreidel
seeds	CD

CD-ROM	camera
cassette	sunglasses
flute	baseball
recorder	toothbrush
magnet	glow-in-the-dark skeleton
game board and pieces	snow globe
timer	flashlight
blankie	magnetic letters/numbers
plush toy	mittens
puppet	

PACKAGING A NOVELTY BOOK

If your idea requires a special feature, an important challenge is the packaging of the book. When the feature is not one that can be bound into the book—as, for instance, a sheet of Band-aids could be—you must consider how to make the package both secure and enticing. You don't want the book and its added feature to get separated at the store. At the same time, it is important that the package appear inviting. Some books, like cloth books and bathtub books, cannot be shelved like other books, so consider how these could best be displayed.

There is another time when special packaging should be part of your thinking. The terms "picture book" and "storybook" are often used interchangeably. However, they are really two different things. A picture book is generally a single story with pictures on every page. A storybook is a single book with several stories inside and may have a picture on each page or may be more sporadically illustrated. Authors often have ideas for creating several related stories and prefer to have the stories published all together. The storybook is certainly the most efficient way to accomplish this goal. However, storybooks are bigger, contain more type and fewer pictures and generally appear somewhat more intimidating than picture books. That is when inventive ideas for packaging all the books together can make sense.

Blister pack: The book and other items are encased in a plastic shell that is glued to a cardboard backing. The book cover can be clearly seen, and the add-on is also usually a flat item, such as a cassette tape.

Box: A book with a plush toy or other large add-on is usually sold in a cardboard box with a cellophane window. Such boxes come in all shapes and sizes but have the disadvantage that shoppers cannot open and peruse the book. (This is one reason why publishers reserve this treatment for books that are already well known.)

Carrying case: Several related books may be packaged together in a box with a handle. Such a case can be made of any material and can close completely with a buckle, like the deluxe set of Beatrix Potter's stories published by Frederick Warne & Co., or can be open and thematically related to the books, like a cardboard doghouse with little books about several puppies.

Poly-bag: This is a soft plastic bag usually sealed with a cardboard header that gives information about the book. This treatment is usually reserved for cloth books, bathtub books or other books that are not stiff enough for shelf display and must be suspended from hooks in the store rather than displayed on shelves.

Shrinkwrap: Shrinkwrap is probably the most pervasive form of packaging for books with special features. It is a form-fitting plastic coat that covers the book and its add-on and keeps them together in a close embrace. Shrinkwrap has one tremendous disadvantage in that it impedes the prospective purchaser from leafing through the book before buying. Unless the bookseller is willing to open a copy for perusal by customers, or unless the title and cover clearly convey maximum tantalizing information about the book, shrinkwrap may create a strong disincentive to buying.

Slipcase: A slipcase is a cardboard sleeve that holds several books together or may hold together a book with a CD or other flat component. Maurice Sendak's *Nutshell Library* is an example of books sold together in a slipcase.

Tray: A cardboard tray may provide support and security for books and add-ons that are especially fragile. The tray is essentially a box with one large side missing. Generally the goods are shrink-wrapped into the tray.

Certain types of books, like diaries, secret journals or club annals, may depend for their attractiveness on unique methods of closure.

Books die-cut to resemble mommy's purse, daddy's tool box or items of clothing may also benefit from these features.

lock	Velcro
snap	button
buckle	zipper
clasp	adhesive seal

A very dramatic book proposal was a board book that flattened out into a board with a narrow line gouged into it. The book was packaged with a small wind-up railroad train. When the train was wound up and a little nib placed in the gouged line, the train followed the track all around the scene. The packaging required a small blister pack containing the train affixed to the front cover. One couldn't help wondering whether this was really an idea for a children's book or whether it was really a toy. Still, it was a very inventive format and suggests some interesting mix-and-match ideas.

Vehicle	Environment
train	farm
car	zoo
boat	Milky Way
plane	city streets
pirate ship	underground tunnels
space ship	country roads
Spanish galleon	jungle pathways
biplane	river
stagecoach	mountain passes
circus wagon	hiking trails
ambulance	frontier
tractor	racetrack

Similar ideas are books that open up into theatrical settings, with paper doll characters that can be manipulated to enact the story. One publisher has put together well-known fairy tales with costumes for children to wear in impersonating and possibly acting out the characters. There also are fairy-tale books with finger puppets that allow children to role-play. And Berthe's *The Cajun Gingerbread Boy* features a paper doll of the title character that can be manipulated through slits in the pages of the book. Sometimes the book itself becomes an object to play with or display. Several publishers have done little books die-cut into Christmas shapes with an attached golden string for hanging on the Christmas tree.

These ideas create more interesting ideas of how to format books. Consider the following mix-and-match list:

cookbook	trading cards
spelling book	lock
math book	hair decorations
hide-and-seek story	cookie cutters
walk in the woods	scratch and sniff
baseball book	magnetized words or letters
hair book	lift the flaps
princess story	flash cards
diary	jewelry

Some ideas can be made part of the book in the production process and do not require special packaging. For instance, Marcus Pfister's *Rainbow Fish* books feature a fish with glittery scales on the front cover and throughout the book. The effect is accomplished by the use of special appliquéd material put on during the book production process.

In other cases, the special additional feature or merchandise is entirely separate from the book. The American Girl series of books is sold by itself, and accompanying merchandise is available by mail-order catalog. The books *Stellaluna* and *Verdi* by Janell Cannon are sold by themselves, though the starring characters are available as plush toys that often are sold nearby in bookstores. The author Harriet Ziefert created a series of softcover beginning readers with extra pages bound into the front and back that could be cut into flash cards to reinforce learning the words. Sheets of stickers can be bound into a book in a similar way.

The great success of all these ventures demonstrates the importance of a book idea that stands alone and does not rely on the success of added features for its basic appeal. However, the special feature can be as inherent to the book as the type of ink used to print the story or pictures. Consider these options:

glow-in-the-dark ink
glitter ink
metallic ink
neon color ink
3-D illustrations (the book would be packaged with special glasses, of course!)

Think about unusual materials to use for the cover and binding of your book.

fur	sandpaper
puffy cloth	feathers
leather	vinyl
satin	patent leather
wood	velvet

You can also make two books in one. The editors at Sesame Street once developed a book called *I'm My Mommy*. But if the reader flipped the book over, the title was *I'm My Daddy*. The book was really two books—half about mommy, half about daddy. The reader read one half, then turned the book around and read the other half. Another inventive approach is the "flip book." Small drawings in the lower corners of the pages turn into an animated or moving image when flipped quickly by the reader.

And think about distinctive page formats that complement your book idea. Books can be set up to incorporate ideas like these:

- slit pages to allow a character to "run" through the story
- fold-out frieze to be decorated with stickers
- mix-and-match pages split horizontally, so different heads can sit on different bodies
- envelopes or mail slots with tiny letters to go inside
- paper model components that can be detached and built
- spaces to write in
- maze
- blank space for child's picture to be pasted

After children graduate from picture books, they are really reading on their own and are moving away from the novelties and toy book concepts. Easy-to-read books feature limited vocabulary, high-interest subject matter, repetition, simple sentence structures. The stories can be like picture books in featuring anthropomorphic animal characters or they can be clearly more sophisticated, featuring mystery stories or nonfiction topics. Ordinarily, the books feature some pictures, but the pictures are a less important part of the overall experience. In fact, the pictures are often in black-and-white and sprinkled intermittently throughout the text.

Even for older children, some novelties can be appropriate. Anything that can be done in the printing process—embossing or printing in a fifth color on covers, or leaving spaces to write in—can be inviting even for older readers. A comic-book format for illustrations can also be appealing. However, books for older readers often look very much like books for adults. Hardcovers with jackets, softcovers with colorful covers—the paper stock, binding and other variables become less important. No matter what age children your book is for, the package is important.

BOOK COVER

Publishers know that the most important ingredient in selling your book is the cover. The writer should think about the cover, too, and be sure there is an irresistible scene or element in the story to feature on an attractive cover. Be ready to discuss commercial cover ideas with the publisher. Although art directors often have their own ideas, your thinking about the commercial appeal of your book may enhance your writing and will certainly impress, and perhaps influence, your publisher. Here are some of the most appealing pictorial elements you can show on the cover. Your story should feature at least one of these items plausibly so that you know an attractive, commercial cover is possible.

interesting main character
unusual setting
holiday symbols
Christmas tree

Easter basket
Hanukkah menorah
Thanksgiving turkey
well-known characters
Santa Claus
Easter Bunny
Pilgrims
cute, familiar animal
baby
princess
grandparents
fairy
cozy home
appealing toy

If you are writing for older children, have a sense of the most appealing visual elements in your story. The cover will look different from the cover for a picture book. It will be more like the cover for an adult novel. Here are a few ideas.

attractive hero/heroine
sports paraphernalia
exchange of romantic looks
suspense indicators (dark, fog, etc.)
car
glamorous clothes
work uniform
trendy clothes
urban setting

BOOK TITLE

Work hard on an alluring title. Although the title is one aspect of your book that is likely to change at least once during the publishing process, a good title can help you grab an editor's attention. Here are some magic words to include in your title for younger children:

Christmas	bunny
Santa Claus	kitten

puppy	counting
baby	shapes
Grandma/Grandpa	colors
big (bigger, biggest)	dinosaurs
best	tiny
busy	stars and planets
good night	naughty
ABC	little

Here are some magic words in titles for older children:

mystery	treasure
kiss	pest
war	king
planet	trouble
secret	midnight
magic	summer
spy	home

If you think your book may still need a little extra help, think about other information that could be printed on the cover as a subtitle, tag line or logo. Thinking of your own book, fill in the blanks below to determine the types of information that can be effectively communicated in this manner.

A Story About _____

A Book About _____

Poems About _____

Will (character's name) be able to (universal or sympathetic goal)?

Fun Facts and Figures About _____

A _____ Book

A _____ Story

All About _____

By thinking about the packaging of your book, you can help it become a strong seller!

BOOKS FOR OLDER READERS

As children grow older, book formats change to emphasize text over pictures. Moreover, novelties cease to be an important feature of the book landscape. These developments occur as children become more comfortable with books and reading and increasingly turn to books for information and enlightenment rather than basic learning and fun. Here are the primary book formats for children over age seven or eight.

Easy-to-read books: These hardcover or softcover books, usually forty-eight pages with some illustrations, are designed to bridge the gap between picture books and middle-grade books. An easy-to-read (or reader) reinforces a child's burgeoning reading skills by presenting several brief stories written with controlled vocabulary and frequent word repetition. The pictures are not always full-color illustrations and usually take up less space on the page than the text. Type is big and readable and broken up into short lines for ready comprehension. The vertical dimensions of the typical reader page accommodate this type layout.

Famous examples of readers are Arnold Lobel's books about Frog and Toad, Else Holmlund Minarik's books about Little Bear, and Peggy Parish's Amelia Bedelia books. Dr. Seuss's books are probably the finest flowering of readers because they break the formulaic mode and are such fun to read that children don't have a clue of the important reading skills they're deriving from the funny, funny texts. Nonfiction subjects also work well in the reader format.

Chapter books: The next step in reading is chapter books. Chapter books are slightly longer than readers, perhaps sixty-four pages or more, and the page design and dimensions are more horizontal. The type is still large, with plenty of space between the words and lines. However, the lines are longer and flow together, an advance on the short, artificially broken lines in readers. Generally a chapter book will tell one story, but the story is broken up into chapters to provide the target audience with manageable units of reading that let him gauge his progress through the book and achieve a sense of accomplishment with each chapter finished.

Carolyn Haywood's Betsy series, Robert McCloskey's *Homer Price,* and Donald Sobol's books about Encyclopedia Brown fall into the chapter-book category.

Middle-grade books: Now children begin to read books that truly resemble the novels read by their parents, though the children's books are generally shorter. In addition, middle-grade fiction published in paperback is often published in a wider size than the rack-sized paperback favored by adolescents and adults. The wider page again allows for a bigger, more readable type size with good spacing between words and lines. Books in this category generally contain page counts of ninety-six pages or more and are divided into chapters, though the divisions are more organic here than in the somewhat choppier chapter books. Children reading middle-grade books may begin to be hooked on series with ongoing characters and situations. Often the characters in these books are the same age as or are slightly older than the target readers and have realistic adventures or experiences.

Beverly Cleary's Ramona books are perfect examples of middle-grade fiction. Ann M. Martin's Baby-Sitters' Club books constitute an age-appropriate series for middle-grade girls.

A WORD ABOUT SERIES

Particularly with books for older children, the most visible successes are often series—even among easy-to-read books, there are several Frog and Toad volumes, several Little Bear books and so on. With very few exceptions, successful series always start with one book that exceeds expectations and thus calls forth others in its wake.

As a writer, you may have an idea for a series for these older readers. However, as an aspirant seeking publication, you must succeed first in interesting the publisher in one book. Focus your attention on developing one manuscript with many attractive elements. Once a publisher demonstrates interest, you can begin to uncover your ideas for a series.

Very occasionally, a series is envisioned at the outset of publication (in the case of Nancy Drew, for instance). However, this is the exception rather then the rule. And in today's cautious climate, it would be very difficult to interest a publisher in making the large up-front investment required for multivolume publication of an untried property.

Young adult (YA) books: Young adult books are closest to books for adults in size, shape and content. Though generally shorter than most adult novels, these books resemble their older cousins in type size and page layout. Vocabulary may also be quite close to that found in books for grown-ups. The principal distinction between adult fiction and young-adult fiction is that the latter features young people in the principal roles. Moreover, the plots develop situations peculiar to adolescents and of greatest interest to that audience. Some of the famous books in this category feature frank depictions of sexual situations, drug use, eating disorders, mental illness and family pathologies that may help young people recognize and deal appropriately with difficult situations in their own lives.

There are many, many well-known YA books. Some authors to sample are Judy Blume, Richard Peck, Madeleine L'Engle, Walter Dean Myers, Gary Paulsen, and Louis Sachar. There are also numerous successful YA series, like Sweet Valley High and Animorphs.

Categories and Genres

Like adult books, middle-grade and YA books may be typed by genre, or kind of story. It may help reach a publisher to be able to apply one of these tags to your book.

Romance: A romance is a book that emphasizes love interest, usually involving male and female protagonists from different backgrounds or a male love object who is mysterious or unobtainable. In the juvenile context, a new boy at school or a popular boy loved by a shy girl may satisfy the requirements for the hero. Generally, success eventually attends the heroine's efforts to connect with her beloved. Getting asked to the dance would constitute a happy ending in a middle-grade romance. For adolescents, romance can touch on serious themes, including peer pressure and war. Bette Greene's *Morning Is a Long Time Coming* is an example. Some aspects to consider if you want to write romance for young people:

starting at a new school
rivalry with another girl
"in" group/"out" group
getting information about love object (from his friends, sister, etc.)

rivalry with love object that ripens into attraction (e.g., cocaptains of debate team)
gifts/tokens (friendship bracelet/anklet)
separation (e.g., summer vacation, winter break)
changing appearance to heighten attraction
developing interests to enhance compatibility
fixing up friends
secret crush

Action/adventure: An action/adventure story often begins with an incident that lands the protagonist in unexpected circumstances. For instance, an airplane crash or boating accident may leave the young heroine stranded in the wild; or finding out a family secret may create challenging situations. The principal feature of such stories is that the protagonist must use his or her wits to come out of the situation safe as well as smarter and more self-assured than before. A classic example is Jean Craighead George's *Julie of the Wolves.* Another acclaimed and popular book is *Hatchet* by Gary Paulsen. Some features to consider in action/adventure stories:

parent is a spy	finding/building hiding place
buried treasure	foraging for food
wilderness	traveling by foot
roughing it	thinking ahead/strategizing
wild animals	navigating by sun and stars
animal companion	telling time by sun
making tools	dangerous stranger
woodcraft	

Mystery: A mystery is a story marked by an unanswered question. The starting place is often a crime or some apparent wrongdoing, and it is unclear who is responsible. The protagonist of a mystery is almost always the detective; in juvenile mysteries this is almost always a child and therefore an amateur who sleuths with the help of friends. Developing unusual powers of observation and exhibiting perseverance, the young detective eventually solves the problem despite several wrong turnings (''red herrings'') in the course of the story. Todd

Strasser writes popular mysteries for young people. *The Accident* is a good example. Aspects of the mystery include:

mysterious newcomer
footprints
fingerprints
torn notes
code
invisible ink
masks and disguises
hair/fiber
tracks
abandoned house
resistance of adults/authority figures
protagonist gets into trouble/is grounded

Suspense/thriller: A thriller is similar to a mystery except that the reader knows all along "whodunit." The question is whether the protagonist, who shares this knowledge, can avoid the wrath/revenge of the wrongdoer. A typical thriller might involve a young person who witnesses a crime and is seen by the perpetrator. The criminal then stalks the young person, who must use his wits to resolve the situation. Caroline B. Cooney has written several such books, including *The Fire.* Some features of the thriller are:

stumbling onto the crime scene
narrow escape
climbing tree
being chased
sneaking around
wearing a disguise or changing appearance
importance of keeping a secret
threats
inability to confide in parents/friends/authorities
being in a forbidden place
being very quiet
hiding out

Sports stories: The sports story tends to feature a talented protagonist who must overcome an obstacle—excessive ego, laziness, prejudice—to make his best contribution to the team. As these books are most often read by children knowledgeable about sports, detailed descriptions of play are *de rigueur*. In addition, such a story will often feature an important game at the climax in which the hero takes an important part. Some element of wish fulfillment, allowing the reader to experience some of the thrill of being a team hero, may be a satisfying part of a good sports story. Sports stories for girls are an increasing feature of this genre's landscape. The books of R.R. Knudson (*Zanballer*) and Matt Christopher (*Return of the Home Run Kid*) are particularly good in this regard.

school playground
pick-up games
trying out for team
rivalry with teammate
rivalry with another school
tough coach
living up to older sibling's/parent's expectations/record
training
bus to away games
cheerleaders
disappointing schoolmates/spectators
injury
strategy
cheating/foul play

Biography: A biography is, of course, the life story of an actual individual. Most such books focus on well-known or significant historical personages. The author may elect to tell the entire life of the subject, or may opt to focus on a particularly important or productive period. Scholarship and accuracy are important, of course. But writers for young people often take greater license in writing biographies than do writers for adult readers. For instance, imagining and including dialogue, or reconstructing unknowable aspects of the subject's childhood, may be legitimate features of the juvenile biographer's craft. Ann Rinaldi's biographies, including *Hang a Thousand Trees With Ribbons* (about the poet Phyllis Wheatley), have been well received.

description of significant places
establishing historical period
tangible details of housekeeping, dress, food, etc.
early education
religious training
travel (means and places)
first accomplishment in field of endeavor
most notable accomplishments
significance of accomplishments and life
if subject is living, future prospects

Science fiction/fantasy: Science fiction/fantasy is a broad category encompassing both stories set in the distant past and stories set in the far future. The common element is that the story occurs primarily in a world of the author's imagining. A book set in the mythical days of Arthurian legend may be a fantasy if it involves magic and wizardry. A book set on another planet in the far future may be a fantasy if the creatures there have evolved powers of their own. Science fiction tends to have more focus on technology–the development of machinery or other systems allowing exploration beyond what we now know and enhancement of human capacities beyond what we can now imagine. In books for young readers, the "time warp" has been a popular device for bringing youthful characters to the past, future or just to a different world. Madeleine L'Engle's trilogy *A Wrinkle in Time, A Swiftly Tilting Planet* and *Many Waters* is an excellent illustration of several ways in which time warp can be used. *Many Waters* is an especially interesting illustration of the fantasy genre. The book is set in Bible times and tells the story of Noah through the eyes of modern teenage twins who accidentally travel to the past. The author imagines an entire society of men and angels living in a desert oasis. The Bible is a point of departure merely; the elaboration of this special world is all the author's invention. Another popular series is the *Time Warp Trio* by Jon Scieszka. The greatest challenge for the writer is to remain absolutely consistent in the depiction of the new world, to set ground rules for some or all of the following elements and stick to them.
description of a distant world

description of another time period
creatures who inhabit this time and place
benign or dangerous creatures
role of humans in this world
enslavement
supremacy
challenge to order existing in fantasy world
multiple suns/moons
means of travel through space and/or time
mental faculties evolved to allow unusual perception
      or experience
role of emotion
interaction of different classes of being
role of gravity or other natural forces
supernatural forces/beings/powers
climatic or other natural catastrophe
witchcraft/wizardry
prophecy/prediction

True crime: This genre may be one of the less developed for young readers. In a true crime book, the author provides the anatomy of a crime that really happened. The crime should be one of special interest, perhaps a very high-profile incident like the kidnapping of the Lindbergh baby. Some subjects that have been covered in juvenile books include a prison break from Alcatraz, presidential assassinations and hate crimes. There is an element of muckraking in books of this nature, but they can also serve the constructive purpose of discouraging antisocial behaviors through example.

famous criminal/victim
well-known incident
interviews with eyewitnesses/participants
explanation of how it was done
background of criminal
motive of criminal
earlier criminal involvement
special nature of victim or object of crime
planning

means used
accomplices
weapons
evading authorities
hiding out
first suspicions
discovering the crime
investigation
first lead
other suspects
path to true culprit

Historical fiction: Painstaking research is the hallmark of books written in this genre. As opposed to fantasy books, these books are set in the documented past. They may feature some historical characters, as in Mark Twain's *The Prince and the Pauper,* Esther Forbes's *Johnny Tremain* or Joan Elizabeth Goodman's *The Winter Hare,* or they may be entirely fictional from the point of view of character and incident but accurately depict historical conditions and lifestyles, as in Berthe's *Lost Magic.* Historical fiction for young readers usually tells of a historical moment as experienced by a young character with whom readers can relate. Although living conditions may vary from one period to another, human emotions do not change much and should be believable. However, it is important to guard against anachronisms, especially in the characters' speech. Overly casual or careless dialogue will not sound right in the mouths of Victorian characters, no matter how *au courant* their feelings.

description of a place in that time
political situation
warring sides or factions
shifting loyalties
divided families
dress
food people ate
how they washed
class structure
hierarchy in seating at table

arranged marriages
epidemics and plagues
wars and causes of wars
hegemony of the Church
religious/political tolerance/persecution
the time in science and medicine
degree of literacy
methods of education
torture
architecture

Horror: A horror story usually involves a terrifying supernatural force or creature that targets the protagonists. The supernatural being may be a vengeful individual returned from the dead, a creature combining human and animal traits (e.g., a werewolf) or even an inanimate object imbued with an evil spirit. The power may be unleashed by natural forces, such as the moon in the case of a werewolf, or it may be the result of tampering with the natural order. Dr. Jekyll's potion is an example of the latter type of horror story. Horror stories are perhaps most compelling when the horror resides in an otherwise normal-seeming individual and is released through some unusual series of events. Popular horror authors for young people include R.L. Stine and Christopher Pike.

devil	spells
voodoo	amulets
evil spirits	incantations
ghosts	book of spells
potion	cauldron
reviving the dead	exorcism
changing shape / form	snakes
electrical storm	pagan idols
Black Mass	evil dolls
witchcraft	

Animal stories: All the genres discussed so far are popular with adult readers and with young readers. By contrast, animal stories are found almost exclusively in books for young readers. Although anthropomorphic animals are most often encountered in picture books for the very young, novels with animal characters have been very popular with young readers over the years. Kenneth Grahame's *The Wind in the Willows* may be the best-known example, but E.B. White's *Charlotte's Web* and Robert Lawson's *Rabbit Hill* are two more classic examples. Robert C O'Brien's *Mrs. Frisby and the Rats of NIMH* is a modern model, and George Selden is another timeless author in this vein. Animal stories for older readers may be more or less realistic but must present a consistent world for the animal characters to inhabit. Thus, in *Charlotte's Web*, the animals Wilbur and Charlotte can talk to one another, and the human girl Fern can talk to her parents, but the animals and the humans do not talk to one another. The realism of the story is so consistent, matter-of-fact and credible that the reader can actually believe it when the curtain between the two worlds drops and Charlotte communicates verbally with the human world.

farmyard	perilous journey
threat to animals	encounters with humans
encroaching humans	evading natural (animal)
slaughter	enemies
moving away	finding home/family
habitat	danger
food	

In writing genre fiction it is important you remember the age of your audience. You may choose to test the limits of acceptable material but should be aware that editors, librarians, teachers and other influential adults may disapprove of your book and have a negative impact on children's access to your work. Most mysteries for young people do not involve murders, and most horror stories do not involve undue gore. This type of writing allows you to elaborate complex ideas in a satisfying way; but always keep in mind the special nature and needs of your young audience.

Chapter Four

Characters

Kids! Cats! Elves! Just as children's books allow you lots of scope in choosing your format, they give you a rare opportunity to be creative with your cast of characters as well. Of course, most books have human characters, and this may be true of children's books as well. But children's books often feature animal characters who think and behave like humans, or fantasy characters like witches and goblins. Often children's books feature combinations of different kinds of characters, although mixing animal, human and supernatural characters takes some very special writing skills. Here are a few factors to consider when you want to mix human and animal characters:

how they communicate
where they live
what they wear
lifestyles
family groupings
what they eat
how they earn a living
how they raise young
wild or domesticated animals
benevolent or cruel people

When working with supernatural creatures and humans, think about some of these questions:

- Are the supernatural creatures visible?
- How do they make their presence known?
- Where did they come from and why?

- Do they have their own language?
- Do they have any special powers?

Writers answer these questions in their own ways, and the answers are far from consistent. Although the accepted wisdom is that animal characters may speak among themselves but not with human characters in a realistic setting, many outstanding books have broken this rule. For instance, in *The Wind in the Willows*, Mr. Toad interacts and converses with a human washerwoman, constable and jailer's daughter. However, it may be important to note that Toad has wandered far from his all-animal society at the points in the narrative where the encounters take place. In Hugh Lofting's *The Story of Dr. Dolittle* and its sequels, the author mines the conceit of a veterinarian who learns to converse in the animals' languages. The lesson is that you cannot ignore this issue but must find a novel and satisfying solution.

The human beings in children's books are most often the types of people children encounter in their everyday lives—playmates, parents, teachers. However, human characters are not always realistic or placed in realistic situations. Mirette in Emily Arnold McCully's *Mirette on the High Wire*, Max in Maurice Sendak's *Where the Wild Things Are*, and Harold in Crockett Johnson's *Harold and the Purple Crayon* are seemingly ordinary children who have exceptional experiences. None of the authors tells much about the protagonist, rather allowing the character's personality to emerge through the action. We learn that the heroes are quirky, intrepid souls who can provide children with role models for conquering fears.

Mirette, Max and Harold are not what classic literary criticism would call fully rounded characters. Fully rounded characters have complex psychology and motivations, and their inner conflicts spur the action. Children's picture books are so brief that usually the author can explore no more than one or two aspects of a character. Still, character is always the springboard for convincing action: The conflict between one individual character's duty and desire makes the story happen. Think about Kay Thompson's *Eloise*—the main character is obligated to live at the swanky Plaza Hotel, an environment devoid of other children and with seemingly few sources of childlike amusement. But Eloise has the desire to be a playful, mischievous child. The story is ignited by the friction between her circumstances and her personality.

The following mix-and-match list provides examples of character traits common to children and duties or obligations that may produce story-generating tension:

shy	go to a party
adventurous	go to school
funny	care for a sibling
loud	care for a pet
quiet	exhibit manners
brave	return lost property
frightened	go to sleep
slow	get dressed
fast	concern for safety
grumpy	move away
independent	take responsibility
sad	help mother
happy	obey parents
angry	go to the doctor

Establishing an inner conflict that makes your story happen means understanding your characters' psychology and motivations, but it also means understanding certain logistical things about your characters—age, physical characteristics, setting. You can refer to chapter one for insight into children's physical abilities and characteristics at particular ages. However, a child may have a limited range of physical abilities and still aspire to do things beyond his capacity. This tension has been the starting point of many children's books.

All your characters will not be rounded characters. In addition to your protagonist, your book will be populated with others who will often be flat characters. These are characters who act upon your hero and to whom the hero reacts. The parent who tells the child not to wander out of the yard, the teacher who warns the child to sit down, the storekeeper who limits the child's choices—these are the vehicles that prompt the main character's conflict. Most often, it is the child character in your book who grows and changes through the action of the story. The other characters need recognizable characteristics but not necessarily all the inner conflict that puts the hero at the center of the book's world.

Nevertheless, if you are writing a contemporary, realistic story, your characters must reflect contemporary reality. By and large, today's grandmothers are not little old ladies with white hair rolled in buns, long flowered dresses, black hose and sensible shoes. They are more likely to be dressed in jogging outfits and sneakers, with youthful hairstyles, makeup and jewelry. Nowadays, with life expectancies on the rise, children are increasingly likely to have great-grandparents living. A great-grandmother or great-grandfather may be more likely to adhere to the old-fashioned stereotype than modern grandparents.

Likewise, schoolteachers are not prim spinsters with disapproving expressions. They are, more often, young, lively, attractive, interested in the development of children's innate abilities as much as in imparting information. And often they are men! Of course, the old-fashioned stereotypes of these stock characters can be exploited for humor or satire. Moreover, if you are writing a story set in the past, exploiting the older view of certain stock characters may be part of your story's realism. But it's important to be aware of contemporary realities in imagining your cast of characters for a modern story.

PORTRAYING ADULTS

Here are some lists contrasting the traditional view of adult characters in children's books with a more contemporary slant.

Mother

Then	*Now*
stayed home	goes to work
wore apron	wears a business suit
cooked meals	shares chores

Father

Then	*Now*
went to work	shares child care

wore business suit	wears jeans
worked with tools	does housework

Grandparent

Then	*Now*
was retired	goes to work
wore old-fashioned clothes	wears modern dress
made quaint crafts	plays sports

Teacher

Then	*Now*
was a woman	may be a man
wore prim clothing	dresses youthfully
had censorious demeanor	has open outlook

The adults in children's lives may have a wider range of characteristics than those formerly encountered in children's books. Books are no longer restricted to depicting the white, Christian, heterosexual nuclear family of Eloise Wilkin's picture books. Other adult characters in today's books may be:

Parents

parent's same-sex partner
mixed-race/mixed-religion parents
stepparents
chemical-dependent parents
ill parents
single parents
teenage parents

Teachers

soccer coach	ballet master/mistress
violin teacher	tennis pro
piano teacher	tutor
dance instructor	swimming coach/instructor

Health-Care Professionals

doctor	dentist
nurse	optometrist
optician	orthodontist
psychiatrist	specialist

Nonparental Caretakers

au pair	neighbor
nanny	day-care worker
housekeeper	social worker

PORTRAYING DISABILITIES/DISEASE

Keep in mind that all children are not well children, and that children with disabilities or chronic ailments need books, too. Also, their stories can touch and inspire well children. In addition, characters with special needs may be part of populating your fictional world with a variety of real people, or you may find that a well child's interaction with an impaired child or adult produces good story ideas. You must be especially accurate and sensitive in your depiction of conditions or illnesses or conditions like the following:

Blindness: A child may be born blind or may become blind due to disease, trauma or degenerative condition.

Cerebral palsy: This condition is a result of a birth defect. The sufferer's mental capacity is unaffected, but she is subject to uncontrollable muscle spasms.

Cystic fibrosis: This hereditary disease affects both the digestion and respiration. An individual with this condition may have a hearty appetite but his body is unable to process food normally. Bronchial infections are another feature of this disease.

Deformity: Missing or abnormal extremities or limbs may result from birth defects or from accident.

Diminutive/excessive size: These conditions are generally hormonal in nature.

Disfiguring birthmark: Prominent skin discoloration is the most obvious example.

Eating disorders: These illnesses, often generated in conjunction with emotional distress relating to self-image, may result in the sufferer's not eating (anorexia nervosa) or bingeing and expelling food through self-induced vomiting (bulimia). These ailments may be most prevalent among adolescent girls.

Epilepsy: A chronic convulsive disorder that often begins in childhood and may involve loss of consciousness.

Hearing impairment: From moderate to profound deafness. The cause may be congenital or traumatic.

Hemophilia: A hereditary condition in which the sufferer's blood does not clot normally.

Learning differences: There are several kinds of differences receiving serious attention today. Dyslexia, which affects reading and writing ability, and attention deficit with hyperactivity disorder (ADHD), affecting ability to concentrate, are two receiving close scrutiny.

Mental slowness: The sources of retardation can be congenital, a result of brain damage during birth or caused by environmental factors. There are numerous specific conditions, such as Down's syndrome (organic) and autism (possibly partially environmental), and the careful author should research them.

Muscular dystrophy: This disease takes several different forms, but all involve muscle weakness and degeneration. Muscular dystrophy may be congenital or may develop during childhood and most often afflicts the extremities.

Obesity: This condition may be hormonal or may have a significant emotional component.

In creating characters with these or similar challenges, remember to consider and research such factors as the following:

wheelchair
brace
walker
cane
crutch
medication
surgery
physical therapy
talk therapy

handicapped accessibility
special vehicle
    van
    bus
    self-propelled wheelchair
special institutional settings
    hospital
    school
    therapeutic facility
    gymnasium
    swimming pool
    whirlpool
caretaker
    family member
    paid companion
    therapist
    speech pathologist
    audiologist
    physician
    psychiatrist

All the potential characters discussed previously presuppose a contemporary, fictional book. If you choose to write about other eras or places, of course you should create characters who fit into those worlds. Many of the following character types have been popular in children's books over the years. Please keep in mind that all these categories may be gender neutral, and the roles may be filled by male or female characters:

pirate	firefighter
clown	mail carrier
cowhand	zookeeper
monarch (king/queen)	fisher
young royalty (prince/	deckhand
princess)	bandit
farmer	athlete
shepherd	truck driver
police officer	astronaut

PORTRAYING GENDER

Of course, all roles are not gender neutral. Here are several that are always gender specific, at least as the world is presently constituted:

nun	maid
priest	big-league ballplayer
knight	witch

In writing about other times and other places, you may need to be sensitive to gender-specific roles for different occupations. In addition, there may be nuances to the roles the sexes play in the world you choose for your setting. For example, in the world of Judaism, a number of women have been ordained as rabbis for service in Reform temples and several for pulpits in Conservative synagogues. However, women rabbis are still unknown in the world of Orthodox Judaism; similarly with various sects of Christianity.

Your interest may lead you to research groundbreaking historical figures, as Emily Arnold McCully did in *The Pirate Queen,* the story of a real-life pirate queen. You can also imagine a world where some of these barriers will be broken, as in a story set in the future about the first woman pitcher in the major leagues. Here are some characters not yet cast as women in the real world. Will your character be the first?

President	NFL quarterback
Vice President	heavyweight boxing
Mayor of New York	champion
Chief Justice	Catholic priest
Yankee pitcher	

PORTRAYING MULTICULTURALISM

In the last several years, publishers have put a tremendous emphasis on multicultural books—books that reflect non-Eurocentric experiences. Such books reflect the increasingly diverse makeup of the reading public. They also validate a wider range of experiences than one used to find in children's books. And they fit in with school and library collections, where information about other peoples and cultures can take on real importance, both to reinforce curriculum goals and to encourage reading across the population served. The multicultural emphasis provides a lot of opportunity for your exploration of different characters and their experiences.

When you think about your characters in terms of ethnicity and religion, don't limit yourself. There are many different cultures, all with interesting histories and features. So, for instance, when thinking about Asian-American characters, you can explore beyond people with roots in China, Japan or Korea, and think about people with origins in the Philippines, Thailand, Laos, Cambodia, Vietnam, Nepal, Tibet, India, Pakistan, Bangladesh, Myanmar, Bali, Indonesia or Malaysia. Many Black Americans have roots in Africa and the American South; but many also have roots in the Caribbean, where culture and history are very different. There is also a wide variety of religions to consider beyond traditional Protestantism, Catholicism and Judaism: Islam, Seventh-Day Adventists (Jehovah's Witnesses), Sikhs, Hinduism, Church of Jesus Christ of Latter-day Saints (Mormons), Buddhism, Shintoism. Religion may affect many aspects of your characters' everyday lives. Be sure you accurately research and convey the following issues:

dress
food
special days of observance
fast days
feast days
intermarriage
treatment of parents
reverence for ancestors/dead
initiation ceremonies
priests or others officiating at ceremonies
religious education of young
special languages for religious observance (e.g., Latin, Hebrew)
cultural aspects
ritual objects
place of worship
religious symbols

form of prayer
sacred texts/books

Another possible cast of characters involves religious figures from the Bible, the Calendar of Saints or other sources. Such individuals can be inspiring role models and impart valuable lessons through children's books. However, treating of such characters requires careful research and respectful presentation. Start with the Bible, if that is your source, and try not to depart from the accepted version of your story. However, it would be most effective to make the character truly a character, with thoughts, feelings and dialogue that reflect real feeling and that children can recognize. Here are some religious figures who may make especially interesting figures in children's books:

Daniel: Sent into exile as an adolescent, Daniel becomes the king's favorite until the envy of the courtiers causes the king to throw him into a den of lions.

Jesus: Accounts of Jesus's life begin with his birth and include many incidents from his life as a young child and growing boy, demonstrating exceptional wisdom and powers beyond his years.

Joan of Arc: Beginning life as a peasant girl, Joan's extraordinary faith and courage soon placed her at the head of the French army, repelling British invaders.

John the Baptist: Often depicted as Jesus's childhood playmate, John was Jesus's cousin who announced his advent.

Joseph: The second youngest of twelve brothers, Joseph has dreams of greatness. Abused by his brothers, Joseph nevertheless realizes his dreams and is reunited with his family.

King David: His story, found in the Books of Samuel I and II, starts when he is a lowly shepherd boy and continues with his glorious reign as King of Israel.

King Solomon: Starting as a young person, King Solomon matures into a great and wise king, solving the difficult problems of many of his subjects.

Mary: The mother of Jesus, Mary's life as a young girl of exemplary virtue has been the subject of many legends.

Moses: Hidden as a baby, Moses is adopted as a foundling into the royal household of Egypt. He grows to lead his people to the Promised Land.

Pope Joan: This legendary medieval figure may actually have lived and been the first and (so far) only woman Pope.

Saint Bernadette: A simple, uneducated young peasant, Bernadette had a vision that established her unusual faith and inspired multitudes of pilgrims.

Some features to look for and emphasize in stories about actual religious figures include the following:

childhood
parentage
family life
early training
first significant religious experience
selection/prediction of greatness
further education/preparation
trials testing faith
exceptional prowess/fortitude
naysayers' doubts/jealousy
communication with the divine
communication of religious verities to others
special skills/abilities
growing up
major accomplishment
profession of faith inspiring others

Here are some examples of ideas for multicultural stories and stories with ethnic characters:

Native American

reservation life	nature lore
tribal gathering	traditional crafts
ceremonial regalia	running races
legends	horses
drums	

African American

Kwanzaa	Southern-style food
church going	basketball
extended family	matriarchal families
slavery days	Islam
choir singing	Southern Baptist religion
Civil Rights era	

Hispanic American

salsa music	Catholic church
Spanish language	bodega
Caribbean food	identifying with place of origin
(plantains, yellow	emigration
rice)	soccer

Asian American

nuclear family	gardens
family council	Buddhism
traditional dress	calligraphy
distinctive foods (rice)	refugee status
arts and crafts (e.g.,	internment
origami)	

Poignant story ideas may arise from the need or effort to assimilate to the majority culture, shedding some distinctive ethnic ways in order to "fit in." Others may be suggested by important historical moments in the collective lives of different ethnic groups, for instance, the internment of Japanese Americans during World War II.

ANTHROPOMORPHIC CHARACTERS

One potential problem with creating very particular human characters is that they may limit the appeal of your book. Your book about same-sex parents is likely to be most appealing to families confronting that particular issue; similarly with books featuring characters of very specific ethnic and religious backgrounds. One way to create a more universally appealing book, especially for younger children, is to fill your cast with anthropomorphic characters.

In chapter three, we explored the many format options open to children's book writers—broad, creative options that are not open to writers of books for adults. You also have more options open to you in choosing the cast of characters for your book. Children's books often feature characters that are rarely the protagonists in adult books, the most common being anthropomorphic animals. As one children's writer has suggested, anthropomorphic animals are people dressed in animal costumes. This author's characters walk on two legs, gesture with their "hands," wear clothes and sleep in beds. However, as discussed below, animal characters may be realistic in appearance and behavior but have some human thoughts and feelings.

The idea of anthropomorphic characters may have started in the days of myth and legend. The Greek myths feature such prodigies of nature as the centaur (half man, half horse), the satyr (half man, half goat) and the sphinx (half woman, half lion). Later, as fairy tales evolved, there developed characters like the bear in the Grimms' "Snow White and Rose Red." Truly an enchanted prince, the character's gruff and frightening appearance is intended to set off his natural goodness and fine breeding. The use of the character here helps convey the message that beauty is more than skin deep, or that even the best of men has something of the beast in him. You can see how the choice of animal characters can be a conscious step in conveying the theme of your story.

An ancient author who had a great hand in developing animal characters is Aesop. In his fables, Aesop exploited the obvious nature and characteristics of different animals. Here are some of the matches Aesop made between animals and their traits. We include a few other examples of "accepted wisdom" that may be worth taking into account in choosing your animal characters.

fox	clever
crow	greedy
rooster	boastful
eagle	kingly

grasshopper	lazy
ant	industrious
beetle	malicious
rabbit	fast
tortoise	slow
dog	dutiful
cat	tricky
lion	strong
mouse	craven
owl	wise
camel	gentle
monkey	foolish
wolf	envious

The apotheosis of the anthropomorphic character is Mickey Mouse. Ostensibly he is a mouse, and he has the snout, big ears and long tail to prove it. But he wears clothes, drives a car, speaks English, lives in a house and does a hundred and one other things that people do. It grabs your attention that Mickey is a mouse, though, doesn't it? He seems cute and vulnerable in a way he wouldn't if he were a little man. At the same time, he seems much more appealing than a real mouse because of his human characteristics.

Anthropomorphic characters sometimes retain more of their nonhuman nature than Mickey Mouse does. The protagonist in *The Velveteen Rabbit* by Margery Williams is a toy. He cannot move by himself, and he is subject to being squeezed too hard, being left out in the garden, being thrown out with the trash. The Velveteen Rabbit is anthropomorphic because he has human thoughts, feelings and aspirations. In every other way, he is a realistic toy (at least until the climax of the story). The duck family in Robert McCloskey's *Make Way for Ducklings* act like real ducks though they have feelings akin to those of people. The little hero in Marjorie Flack's *The Story About Ping* is another ducky example.

Your story is like a movie, and you are the director. You can cast your movie with any characters you like. In any story, it's key to have a good, appropriate cast of characters. In children's picture books, it's also important to have characters who are visually interesting and appealing. Of course, pictures of children can be attractive. But animal characters are at once more whimsical and more exotic.

Why Use Animals?

You may wonder when and why you would choose to have animal characters. The answer is that you may sometimes want them in whimsical situations, or when you can use one of the animal's special traits to illustrate a key concept you wish to convey to children. For instance, if you want to show something about a child learning skills needed in growing up, you could tell the story of a little bear catching his own fish for the first time or staking out the honey tree. Such an experience may subtly tell the child important information about coping with milestones in growing up and fending for himself. Casting a bear in the story helps you convey the message in a fun way, without getting didactic, and may even allow you to communicate some information about bears into the bargain. (Often this will be "light" information, such as that bears like to eat honey and fish.)

Most times your anthropomorphic animal character will be a stand-in for a child character, but the animal costume provides a way to emphasize or even exaggerate a particular characteristic without making the child grotesque or an object of fun. For example, H.A. Rey's Curious George character represents a child who, in all innocence, cannot resist getting into mischief. As a monkey, George can get into much more extreme and amusing situations than a human child plausibly (or safely) could. Still, the point of the stories for human readers is clearly made.

There are other reasons to have anthropomorphic characters. Perhaps the animal's name suggests a funny title, as in Joan Elizabeth Goodman's cat story *The Secret Life of Walter Kitty*, a play on James Thurber's famous title. Or you may have an illustrator who draws animals better than people. You would cast animals in your leading parts for the same reason some film scripts work better as animated films than as live action—you want the characters to be able to do things that human beings ordinarily can't do. But you can also let the animals use their natural attributes to benefit the story. Here is a list of animals with the qualities, homes and characteristics attributed to them by the popular mind. This list could help you choose which animal would be best for your story. Remember that playing around with each animal's attributes in a way that defies the reader's expectations may be a great beginning for your story. For instance, several successful children's books have grown out of the idea of one animal trying out another's usual home.

Animal	Personality Trait	Home	Physical Characteristic
beaver	busy, industrious	lodge, dam	large flat tail
bear	hungry, slow-witted	cave, hollow log	teeth, claws
elephant	long life and memory	jungle	trunk, wrinkly skin
kitten	curious, timid	people's home	big eyes and ears
puppy	playful, mischievous	doghouse	floppy ears, tail
pig	greedy, rowdy	farmyard	pink skin, curly tail
cow	placid	meadow	hooves, horns
lion	brave, threatening	grassland	mane
rabbit	quick, clever	rabbit hole	long ears, cotton tail

You can use anthropomorphic characters for irony and dramatic contrast—think of Ogden Nash's poem "Custard the Dragon." One expects a dragon to be brave, but Custard is a big coward. Even Ink, the mouse, seems braver than he. Still, it is poor Custard who scares off the pirate, discovering his own dragon-y nature. Similarly, the young bull in Munro Leaf's *The Story of Ferdinand* defies expectations by being a peace-loving animal.

It may be fun to write a story about animals who defy expectation by having character different from those one expects. Think about this mix-and-match list:

bull	shy
bear	greedy
chicken	smart
cat	lively
dog	silly
bird	jealous
monkey	sleepy

elephant	cowardly
lion	friendly
giraffe	rowdy
goose	gentle
pig	kind

All animals are not equally appealing as anthropomorphic characters. Overall, mammals and quadrupeds are to be preferred. Generally, appealing animal characters have fur, four legs, big eyes and an identifiable sound. It is a big plus if the animal is one that is well known to children. There is a "top ten" list of animals that work best in picture books, based on the number of titles published using these animals and the popularity of the books:

Good Anthromorphic Characters

bear	mouse
cat	elephant
dog	lion
rabbit	chicken
pig	cow

Other animals that have worked as protagonists in stories are:

monkey	toad
aardvark	crocodile
gopher	hippopotamus
prairie dog	mole
hedgehog	donkey
duck	penguin
chicken	moose
frog	

Generally, stay away from animals that are unfamiliar or repellent, including most rodents, insects, crustaceans and reptiles. Some that do not work are:

| cockroach | lobster |
| rat | flea |

alligator	ferret
worm	weasel
gnat	mink

Of course, there are exceptions to these rules. The heroine of Janell Cannon's *Stellaluna* is a bat, not exactly a cuddly or adorable animal. But *Stellaluna* features spectacular artwork that goes a long way toward making the heroine palatable. The same author managed a similar feat with her book *Verdi*, the story of a snake. There are also subtle distinctions to be made: For example, a worm probably does not work as a hero for a book. But a cute fuzzy caterpillar that turns into a moth or butterfly may be an appealing character.

If the idea of anthropomorphic animals appeals to you, stay away from ideas that betray the whole concept of the animals. For instance, a story line that requires a turtle character to shed its shell does not work because a turtle cannot live without its shell. Similarly, a story line requiring a carnivorous animals to lose all its teeth doesn't work because such an animal would die. One failed manuscript involved a killer whale who felt unhappy about himself because he had no teeth. But his parents believed in him and taught him he didn't need teeth to get by so long as he used his brain. The author neglected to realize that this message may be true for children but is not true for killer whales. Many writers assume their animal characters can get along even though they're different. This may work for humans, who have all kinds of adaptive capacities; it does not work for animals, which are designed in a particular way because it helps them survive physically. Don't be naive, and don't assume children will relate to your story if it makes no sense or creates an illogical example or encourages them in bad behavior (for instance, seeing whether Tommy the Turtle really can survive without his shell).

Nevertheless, Hans Christian Andersen's story of "The Ugly Duckling" points the way to a productive use of animal characters' natural characteristics to defy expectations. In that story, of course, the protagonist is branded a misfit because he hatches out of one of a clutch of eggs and does not resemble his siblings. It turns out that he was a swan all along. This classic plot line suggests other mix-and-match ideas using an animal's true characteristics to create a lively, convincing and instructive story:

duck	beautiful
caterpillar	loud
butterfly	obedient
cow	small
bear	peaceful
dog	large
cat	smooth
mouse	big-eyed
snake	furry

Other Anthropomorphic Characters

This discussion of anthropomorphic characters has so far assumed the development of naturalistic animal characters living in their natural habitats and exhibiting at least some of their distinctive natural behaviors. However, animal characters can just as easily live in houses, wear clothes, go to school, just like your human characters. In this type of story, the use of animal characters is essentially a kind of window dressing where the animals basically add to the cuteness and appeal of your book.

Anthropomorphic characters of this type may be especially welcome when you are dealing with sensitive, emotional topics, where they may add a touch of welcome fantasy to the otherwise rather serious proceedings. One place to avoid animal characters is religious books, although Jane Breskin Zalben has had success with her books about Beni, a little Jewish bear. However, many parents might be offended at the idea of animals in religious settings. As already noted, it is a plus to anthropomorphic characters that they have no particular race, religion or ethnicity. Thus, children of all backgrounds are able to relate to the book.

Here are some situations where an animal character works well:
first day of school
death of loved one

new baby
growing up
fitting in
night fears
being "different"
    too big
    too little
    different color
    different species
    too loud
    too timid

Anthropomorphic characters are not always animals. They may take all kinds of forms. It is tempting but tricky to make characters of inanimate objects. For instance, the heroes of A.A. Milne's *Winnie-the-Pooh* and Margery Williams' *The Velveteen Rabbit* are toys, not actual animals. The protagonist in Hans Christian Andersen's story "The Little Fir Tree" is, obviously, a tree. Generally, your anthropomorphic character should be based on a living thing. When you build your story around an inanimate object, you make it much more difficult for the reader to believe the character has the thoughts and feelings you ascribe to it. You may also find yourself hamstrung in creating a story with interesting action. After all, rocks and trees mostly stay in one place. Although anthropomorphic characters presuppose some fantasy element to your story, you must observe the ground rules of realism and not test the reader's imagination too far. There are exceptions to the rule, however, and the following is a list of successful books featuring anthropomorphic characters based on inanimate objects.

The Giving Tree by Shel Silverstein

Scuffy the Tugboat by Gertrude Crampton

Tootle by Gertrude Crampton

Little Toot by Hardie Gramatky

Thomas the Tank Engine by Rev. W. Awdry

The Little Engine That Could by Watty Piper

The Little Red Caboose by Marion Potter

The Taxi That Hurried by Lucy Sprague Mitchell, Irma Simonton Black and Jessie Stanton

Budgie the Little Helicopter by H.R.H. the Duchess of York

Pinocchio by Carlo Collodi

Raggedy Ann and Andy by Johnny Gruelle

The Brave Little Toaster by Thomas M. Disch

Think about the commonalities that make these inanimate objects into successful characters. They are almost all toys, vehicles or living (but stationary) things. Toys are a natural because children personify them in the course of play. Moreover, toys often have some features of recognizable human or animal anatomy, so it is not a far stretch to imagine them moving and behaving as people. Vehicles have built-in interest because they can move, travel, seem to have adventures. Living things are also easy to imbue with personality, even if, like trees, they do not move. If you are considering writing a story personifying an inanimate or stationary object, look for these same traits:

mobility
recognizable anatomy
life

Following these criteria, you will find that rocks, buttons, garbage cans and other such items are unlikely to make it as book characters.

There are stories that mix anthropomorphic characters with human or other realistic characters. Margaret Wise Brown's *Mister Dog* and Charlotte Zolotow's *Mr. Rabbit and the Lovely Present* are examples. Hugh Lofting's *The Story of Doctor Dolittle* is a book for older readers but follows the same idea. The writer must take care to respect the boundaries of the reality he has created. If your story features people interacting with animals as if the animals were human beings, you will find it very difficult then to introduce animals behaving in a naturalistic manner, as pets or wild creatures. In Lewis Carroll's *Alice in Wonderland,* Alice is the proud owner of a cat named Dinah. However, the true-to-life Dinah does not accompany Alice down the rabbit hole, where animals behave more like eccentric Victorians. In most instances, you should not cross the boundary between the naturalistic world and the anthropomorphic world.

Audience

Keep in mind that overall anthropomorphic animals may be more at home in your picture-book manuscripts than in your writing for older children, such as chapter books or novels. As children grow older, they become more interested in seeing reality reflected in their reading. Their reading is more purposeful—they want to learn about life as it is. Therefore, anthropomorphic characters become less appropriate as children grow older, although there are some obvious and wonderful exceptions, such as Kenneth Grahame's *The Wind in the Willows,* Richard Adams's *Watership Down* and Robert C. O'Brien's *Mrs. Frisby and the Rats of NIMH.*

Stories with anthropomorphic characters can work for older readers when the themes and content of the stories reflect concepts to which older readers can relate. *The Wind in the Willows* is a social satire with animals standing for human characters. Mr. Toad is a perfect example of the privileged, monied country squire with no strictures and no cares. His lack of responsibility leads him into trouble time and again; yet his charm and sense of adventure are completely winning. To appreciate *Mrs. Frisby and the Rats of NIMH,* young readers must be able to empathize with feelings of duty to family and community and to explore complex issues about experimentation with animals. Thus, although the animal characters make the stories look like material for younger children, the seriousness of purpose and theme demand a more mature reader.

Fantasy Characters

There are other types of characters you can use in children's stories that you would not use in stories for adults. These are not animal characters, but fantasy characters with supernatural characteristics.

You may have first encountered such characters in fairy tales or other types of magical fiction. However, these special beings have roles to play in modern-day stories, especially in picture books and in science fiction and fantasy novels for middle-grade and young-adult readers. Despite their ancient lineage, such creatures have provided inspiration to many writers. Here is a glossary of some of these creatures.

Angels: Angels have different origins and appearances in different traditions. Often they are messengers of God, winged and haloed. Sometimes they are apparitions of the spirits of the virtuous dead.

Devils: The word "devil" may also vary in meaning depending on the tradition whence a particular devil arises. Devils are sometimes described as apparitions of the souls of the wicked dead. They may visit the earth to cause trouble to the living. They are sometimes depicted as horned, tailed, hooved and carrying pitchforks. A devil puts in an appearance in Isaac Bashevis Singer's *Zlateh the Goat.*

Dragons: Dragons are dangerous, scaly beasts, often resembling large serpents or lizards, sometimes winged and fire-breathing. They are generally wicked, kidnapping princesses and hoarding treasure. However, they have also been turned into endearing characters, as in Kenneth Grahame's story "The Reluctant Dragon." A more recent example is Jerdine Nolen and Elise Primavera's *Raising Dragons.*

Elves: Elves are small, fairylike creatures with a mischievous streak. This name is also applied to small boys of the fairy world. Elves sometimes help people in need. When the kindness is returned, good fortune attends the grateful humans. Santa Claus is often described as an elf (for instance, in Clement C. Moore's *A Visit From Saint Nicholas*); however, Santa is clearly much bigger than the average elf.

Fairies: Fairies are often tiny creatures living among flowers or in woodlands. They may ride on insects or other small animals, or they may be able to fly by virtue of their own wings. Fairies traditionally can range in size up to human size, can be solitary or live in groups, and can be male although they are most often depicted as delicate females. In olden times, they were known for their skill at spinning and weaving. For a distinctive contemporary use of fairies in young-adult fiction, see Francesca Lia Block's *I Was a Teenage Fairy.* Some well-known examples of fairies are:

Blue fairy: In Carlo Collodi's *Pinocchio,* a blue-haired child who lives in the woods, saves Pinocchio, and trains his conscience.

Evil fairy: Fairies are not always good, as shown by the evil fairy who curses the princess in the story of "The Sleeping Beauty." The fairy is angered and vengeful when she is not invited to the princess's christening.

Fairy godmother: In "Cinderella," this was originally the spirit of Cinderella's dead mother, who helped the heroine from beyond the grave. In later versions, the fairy godmother is an independent spirit who appears in answer to the heroine's need.

Titania: The fairy queen, an important character in Shakespeare's *A Midsummer Night's Dream,* was married to Oberon, King of the Fairies.

Tooth Fairy: A latter-day invention, she takes the teeth children lose and leaves small gifts in their stead. The Tooth Fairy can appear in a humorous way, as in the book *No Tooth, No Quarter,* by Jon Buller and Susan Schade.

Genies: Monstrous spirits, usually found in stories of the *Arabian Nights,* that can change size and shape. Genies may become enslaved to human masters and must place their supernatural powers at their masters' service. The genie in the tale of "Aladdin" is perhaps the best known.

Ghosts: The incorporeal spirits of the dead, ghosts sometimes return to visit the living. Ghosts are depicted as transparent figures, sometimes dragging chains symbolic of their sins in life. The various ghosts in Charles Dickens' *A Christmas Carol* are perhaps the best known. Ghosts appear more playfully in Halloween stories.

Giants: Giants are humanlike creatures that are very large and strong. They can be good or evil, playful or malevolent. Wicked or monstrous giants are known as *ogres,* an example being the shape-shifter in Charles Perrault's tale of "Puss in Boots" or the giant in "Jack and the Beanstalk." Paul Bunyan is a legendary kindly giant of the American tradition.

Gnomes: Charged with guarding the world's treasures, gnomes are small creatures that live underground.

Goblins: Small, ugly beings that are wicked and work mischief in the world of humans. Rumpelstiltskin is a goblin. For an interesting vision of the goblins' lifestyle, read Christina Rossetti's poem "Goblin Market."

Mermaids: Beautiful young women with fishes' tails, mermaids are known for singing sweetly, sometimes tempting sailors into danger. In some traditions, a captured mermaid may become a woman, marry and bear children, though always wishing to return to her home in the sea. The best known mermaid in children's literature is the heroine of Hans Christian Andersen's "The Little Mermaid," who gives up her magical voice to live with her human lover.

Monsters: Monsters usually combine the features of two or more creatures of the natural world—for instance, a griffin is a monster that has some body parts of a lion and some of an eagle. In the modern day, monsters can be cute and endearing, like some of Jim Henson's Muppets, or the hero of Mercer Mayer's Little Critter books.

Pixies: Pixies are fairylike creatures that dress in green. They are known for leading travelers astray.

Trolls: In the Scandinavian tradition, trolls are hairy creatures with big wide mouths. The only way to get rid of a troll is to give it something to eat. The best-known troll is the one that lives under a bridge in the folk tale "The Three Billy Goats Gruff." Trolls also appear in Jan Wahl's *Peter and the Troll Baby.*

Witches: Originally members of an Earth goddess religion, centuries of tradition have transformed witches into magical, and usually malevolent, hags. Dressed in black with pointed hats, carrying brooms on which they ride, luring children to destruction, witches are often objects of fear. The Wicked Witch of the West in L. Frank Baum's *The Wizard of Oz* is a somewhat grotesque and comical example. But witches have appeared in more good-natured guise and have been featured to humorous advantage in modern books by Roald Dahl and others. Norman Bridwell's *The Witch Next Door* is a good picture-book example. Deborah Hautzig's Little Witch character has sparked fine, humorous easy-to-read books. A different approach is found in Steven J. Simmons's *Alice and Greta: A Tale of Two Witches.*

Wizards: Men with supernatural powers, wizards can understand the language of the animals and trees and can change shape at will. The best-known wizard is surely Merlin, a prominent character in any story about King Arthur. The *un*magical title character in *The Wizard of Oz* is a parody of the classic wizard.

Mythological Characters

Yet another category of character is the mythical or legendary character. These characters, passed down in stories for generations, may reflect elements of fact though their existence remains shrouded in uncertainty. When choosing to include such characters in your work, the lack of verifiable fact frees you to add, subtract and modify characteristics and incidents, though you must remain true to some well-known features in order to satisfy readers devoted to these characters.

Gilgamesh: A king of ancient Babylon with divine lineage, Gilgamesh had superhuman strength and intelligence. His youth and impulsiveness made him a sometimes whimsically cruel ruler. However, through his friendship with the wild man Enkidu and his journey to Utnapishtim, he gains knowledge and insight.

Hercules: The son of Zeus, king of the Greek gods, and Semele, Hercules (or Herakles) was the strongest man alive. When the goddess Hera sent two serpents to strangle the infant Hercules in his cradle, the baby's superhuman strength allowed him to strangle the snakes before they could do him any harm. As penance for an act of violence committed in a state of rage, Hercules was required to undertake twelve impossible feats of strength. Despite his successes, Hercules never was happy in his personal life.

Hiawatha: Son of the moon-maiden Nokomis and the West Wind, Hiawatha was a Native American prince noted for his bravery and his ability to be at one with nature. A skilled hunter, Hiawatha killed only what he could use, and he used as much of the kill as possible. At last, hoping to avoid killing altogether, Hiawatha wrestles with a mysterious stranger who, defeated, imparts the secret of corn. Following the stranger's directions, Hiawatha is able to provide for all his people.

Jason: Jason was a Greek prince whose wicked uncle, planning to usurp the throne, sent Jason on a perilous quest. He was to travel to a far-off land and obtain a precious Golden Fleece guarded by a dragon. Jason gathered a crew of heroes, including Hercules, and set to sea in a ship called the *Argo.* Along the way they encountered Harpies (monsters combining features of women, eagles and serpents) and entered the land of the Amazons (warrior women). In Colchis, Jason enlisted the aid of the princess, Medea, a powerful sorceress. She helped them outwit the dragon and secure the fleece. Jason and Medea later married, though not happily.

Johnny Appleseed: A resident of Pittsburgh, John Chapman had a beautiful apple orchard. As the American frontier pushed west, he got the idea of planting apple trees for the settlers to enjoy. Traveling on foot, he spread apple trees through the Ohio River valley. As the years went on, he became more eccentric in manner and appearance.

King Arthur: King Arthur was the son of a British warlord who became the first king to unify England and the first to establish a code of conduct for knights. Often depicted as a young boy raised in obscurity, Arthur eventually became a ruler more noted for his wisdom and deep feeling than for his physical courage. In this growth he was coached by his tutor, the wizard Merlin. Arthur obtained the magical sword Excalibur, married the beautiful princess Guinevere, and formed the Round Table of brave knights. These knights excelled at fighting pagan invaders and later undertook a quest for the Holy Grail. The stories of their adventures during this quest are a rich part of the Arthurian tradition.

Odysseus: The hero of Homer's *Odyssey,* Odysseus was the king of Ithaca, a small Greek island in the Aegean Sea. He was known for his cleverness and was the mastermind behind the Trojan Horse, the ploy that brought an end to the Trojan War. Having angered the sea god Poseidon, Odysseus wandered the seas for ten years before returning to his home and his faithful wife, Penelope. Along the way, he had adventures with the Cyclops, a dalliance with the sea-nymph Calypso and other fantastic adventures.

Rama: Rama was the Indian god Vishnu in human form. A great king, Rama fought a pitched battle with the evil Ravan. In the course of the battle, Rama enlisted the aid of many allies, including the animals. A striking feature of the story is the long-lasting and faithful love of Rama for his bride, Sita.

Robin Hood: Robin Locksley, son of a woodsman loyal to King Richard the Lion-Hearted, is robbed of his home and lands by minions of the wicked King John, ruling in Richard's place during the time of the Crusades. Enraged by this social injustice, Robin adopts the name Robin Hood and goes to live in the wilds of Sherwood Forest, where he and his band of Merry Men (including Little John, Friar Tuck and Alan-a-Dale) steal from the rich in order to provide for the poor disenfranchised by the actions of an evil government. Robin Hood's archenemy is the Sheriff of Nottingham, loyal to King John. Robin's beloved is Maid Marian, betrothed to one of John's knights. Noted for his daring, Robin Hood is also well known for his exceptional skill in archery.

Sigurd: In the Norse sagas, Sigurd was the grandson of the chief god, Odin. Raised by wicked elves, Sigurd nevertheless has nobility and superhuman powers. He can understand the language of the birds and animals, is invincible except for a weak spot near his heel, and has a magical sword and a helmet that allows him to change shape at will. He marries the demigoddess Brynhild but proves untrue and marries a princess after being given a potion by a treacherous king.

Sir Gawain: One of the best-known of King Arthur's knights, Sir Gawain was noted for his noble birth and fine character. Among his most famous adventures are his bitter rivalry with the monstrous Green Knight, the subject of several children's books. Also well known is his marriage with a hideous old hag who, through his good offices, turns out to be a beautiful noblewoman under an evil enchantment.

When developing stories around well-known mythical or legendary characters, try a different approach. For instance, the Disney studios once cast the story of Robin Hood with animals in all the parts— Robin was a fox! In order to identify an existing character you could develop, and in order to identify good sources for new stories involving that character, think about some of the following issues:

interesting early life
childhood manifestation of well-known characteristic

voyage, journey or quest around which new adventures can be
developed
character's first perception of special destiny
society's first perception of character's special destiny
character's education/training
character's friends/companions

There are some other well-known characters who appear frequently in children's books and about whom there is no "official version." Santa Claus and the Easter Bunny are the best examples of characters known to everyone though existing in countless alternative versions. L. Frank Baum did write a charming book called *The Life and Adventures of Santa Claus*, but even that book cannot claim to represent an orthodox view of the origin and nature of Santa. Generally, Santa is portrayed as a fat, jolly elf, dressed in red with white fur trim, who carries Christmas toys to boys and girls around the world. Sometimes he has eight reindeer with names; sometimes he has an extra reindeer named Rudolph; sometimes he goes up and down chimneys. The orthodox view of Santa is actually a product of the vision embodied in a relatively modern literary work, Clement C. Moore's poem *A Visit From Saint Nicholas*. Because there are no hard and fast rules, you can have fun being creative with Santa. The Easter Bunny and the Tooth Fairy are similar constructs of varying views. See if you can think of any new supernatural characters that could become children's guides to universal experiences. Think about how the creature would look and the powers it would have. How about a fairy or elf for each of these events:

first day of school	illness
going to sleep	getting a pet
wishing	Halloween
birthday	new sibling

Historical Characters

Finally, your characters can be real people. Historical personages have made memorable characters both in picture books and in fiction and nonfiction for older children. Of course, Claude Monet inspired

Christina Bjork's *Linnea in Monet's Garden,* and William Blake provided the inspiration for Nancy Willard's Newbery Medal-winning *A Visit to William Blake's Inn.* By mixing real people with your fictional characters, you can provide children with interesting lessons embedded in colorful, entertaining stories. Think about the following historical characters:

Writers
William Shakespeare
Lewis Carroll
Louisa May Alcott
Laura Ingalls Wilder
Mark Twain
Phyllis Wheatley
Anne Frank
Edgar Allan Poe
Helen Keller
Charles Dickens

Composers
Ludwig van Beethoven
Wolfgang Amadeus Mozart
Johann Sebastian Bach
George Gershwin
John Coltrane
John Lennon
Duke Ellington
Felix Mendelssohn
Fanny Mendelssohn
Clara Schumann
Amy Beach

Artists
Pablo Picasso
Auguste Rodin
Rembrandt van Rijn
Pierre-Auguste Renoir
Michelangelo
Jean-Paul Basquiat

Keith Haring
Claude Monet
Mary Cassatt
Faith Ringgold

Athletes
Babe Ruth
Ty Cobb
Mickey Mantle
Jim Thorpe
Jackie Robinson
Jesse Owens
Hank Aaron
Willie Mays
Mark McGwire
Sammy Sosa
Michael Jordan
Pele
Roberto Clemente
Babe Zaharias Didrikson
Jackie Joyner-Kersee
Kristi Yamaguchi
Venus Williams

Government Figures
Theodore Roosevelt
Queen Victoria
Thomas Jefferson
George Washington
Abraham Lincoln
Tutankhamen
Thurgood Marshall
Davy Crockett
Madeleine Albright
Lindy Boggs
Janet Reno
Prince William

Again, in mining historical figures for ideas, it may help to think about their early lives. Surely the fact that Mozart was a famous child prodigy, touring Europe from a very early age, makes him an especially suitable subject for treatment as a children's book character. Theodore Roosevelt's early determination that he would be President is a feature that makes him especially interesting for a young readership. A historical character's involvement with children may reveal a facet that makes the character interesting to young people. For instance, Lewis Carroll was, in his day, a celebrated and pioneering photographer of children.

Other Characters

Your characters can be people, animals, supernatural beings or historical figures. Or they can be several of these things at once. Take a look at the following list and see if you can drive inspiration from mixing and matching the different character types.

angel	cat
devil	dog
witch	monkey
daddy	dinosaur
knight	mouse
princess	swan
dragon	rabbit
ballerina	alligator
wizard	dinosaur
cowboy	pig

Many children's authors have created wonderful characters by combining character types. In Jean de Brunhoff's *The Story of Babar*, the hero is both an elephant and a king. The freedom to create a character truly out of whole cloth is one of the great opportunities open to you as a children's book writer. Seize the opportunity and make the most of it. But make sure you are truly using your imagination. Some characters have become the juvenile writer's stock-intrade. Some stock characters in young-adult fiction include the following:

Valley girl	*Nerd*
shallow	glasses
pretty	high-water jeans
vain	pocket protector
materialistic	loner
popular	obsessive
boy crazy	secretive

Try not to use stock characters but to make your characters truly distinctive and alive. The genius of the film *Clueless* (also the jumping-off place for young-adult television and book series) is its improvement on the Valley girl paradigm. Although the character of Cher appears to be the Valley girl supreme, her intelligence, moral compass and sense of *noblesse oblige* make her a character both individual and endearing. Don't take stock characters at face value; make them your own. You know you are using a stock character when your character looks, acts and talks just like someone you've seen a hundred times on television. In picture books, chapter books or young-adult novels, strive to make characters that are individual, alive and do surprising things.

The only limitation is your imagination.

Chapter Five

Setting

Settings are as many and varied as you can imagine. Simple or complex, they vary for different ages and are essential in creating different atmospheres. In some cases you may want a specific place in the present (e.g., for problem-solving, young-adult novels). Such places include places where young people spend a lot of time, including places where they live, learn and play. However, young people may also work, go off the beaten path and get into trouble. Thus, a random selection of places where their stories or parts of their stories might plausibly be set could include the following:

school	pool hall
hospital	bar
police station	factory
home	diner
pet store	cinema
garage	wilderness trail
stadium	urban park
locker room	trailer park

FANTASY PLACES

Books for young readers may also take place in the past (e.g., historical novels). You may select a time period when the places where young people went were different from such places today. For instance, you might need to picture your characters in one of the following types of places:

castle	marketplace
dungeon	fair
tower	ship

stable	farm
work house	thatched cottage
charity school	craftsman's workshop
orphanage	monastery

Another type of setting may be a fantasy world. The world you create will vary depending on the type of story you are writing. For example, if you are writing an original fairy tale, you will have to create a convincing fairyland. A science-fiction story also requires the creation of a whole new world, but it will be a very different setting from the one where your fairy characters dwell.

Fairyland

hollow tree	cobweb
ferns	marsh
bracken	flower bed
clearing	cave

Science Fiction

spacecraft	planetary ice cap
atmospheric dome	worm hole
undersea city	Martian canals
control tower	

FAMILIAR PLACES

Settings are all-important to theme and plot development. At its most basic level, setting includes the place where your story takes place and the props that are found there. For instance, in the case of infants and young toddlers, settings will be home-based. Generally, there will be a cozy, familiar ambiance to the following places:

Bedroom

crib	crib toy
mobile	blanket

music box	fairy-tale lamp
window	baby intercom

Kitchen

high chair	bowl
baby spoon	bottle
segmented plate	bib
spill-proof cup	

Other Rooms

playpen	chair
toys	layette
books	baby swing
sofa	pet

Bathroom

tub	soap
basin	shampoo
bath toys	mirror
sponge	comb/brush

As infants grow into toddlers, the range of settings where they may find themselves expands to include:

Playground

swings	sprinkler
jungle gym	seesaw
sandbox	merry-go-round
pail	fence
shovel	grass

Day Care

chairs	mats
tables	plates

cups
milk cartons
learning toys

message board with magnetic
letters

Still later, school and other outside-of-home places become important settings for stories.

School

chalkboard
chalk
eraser
books
bulletin board

cubbyhole
American flag
desk
alphabet wall hanging

Around Town

grocery store
supermarket
department store
restaurant
library
park

theater
post office
parent's office
police station
firehouse
gas station

As children grow physically and spiritually, different places may grow in importance.

Church/Synagogue

pews
organ
hymnals
prayerbooks
stained-glass windows
ark

eternal light
pulpit
Bible
lectern
crucifix
statues of saints

Sports Settings

basketball court
bowling alley

baseball diamond
football field

soccer field	racquet
skating rink	ball
goal	bat
backstop	hoop
tennis court	locker room
net	wrestling mats

Finally, familiar settings may be transformed into places where older children and adolescents have experiences peculiar to their stages of developments. For instance, the school gymnasium may become the scene of a dance, homecoming rally or graduation ceremony through use of some of the following items:

bunting	balloons
tinsel	banner
disco lights	ticket desk
multicolored lights	refreshment table
lectern	punch bowl
folding chairs	bleachers

Of course, other settings will change as children develop, too. The child's bedroom will be transformed through the years from the baby's room to the room of a young adult. The addition of some or all of the following items may aid in this transformation:

posters	bookshelf
wallpaper designs	telephone
curtains/shades	television
bed	stereo
bed-linen designs	toy chest
lava lamp	stuffed toys
desk	collections (rocks, cans, etc.)

In addition, a setting can be mobile and can also change according to the age of the reader or character. A car is one experience for a baby riding in a car seat and a very different experience for a teenager who has just rebuilt an old wreck bought with his own money. As you think about how children of different ages might experience some of these different travel options, try to fill in the scene around the vehicle by thinking about the weather, the physical surroundings, the other people present, etc.:

tricycle	bus
bicycle	limousine
carriage	monorail
stroller	roller coaster
motorcycle	hot-air balloon
airplane	truck
helicopter	riding lawn mower
railroad train	horse
subway train	

To sum up some of the ideas discussed above, here are lists of suggested settings arranged according to age appropriateness:

1-4	4-6	6-8 and 8-10	12-up
home	school	foreign countries	anything
nursery school	vacations	space travel	goes
day-care center	the woods	science fiction	
grandmother's	a farm	early America	
zoo	big city	prehistory	
by the sea	parties	Civil War days	
the garden	nature in the wild	Revolution	
	fantasy worlds	other historical events	
	friend's house	contemporary	
		problem situations	

A particular prop may mean something different depending on its physical context. Review the following mix-and-match list and think about how each prop would work in each different setting:

cobweb	haunted house
flower	garden
tower	Tokyo
great oak	enchanted forest
crater	alien planet

maze	castle
secret passage	ship

We can think of settings as concrete places or situations or they can also be interpreted as ambiance used to create an emotional response in the reader (e.g., ghost stories). In this context, settings can encompass a lifetime, a day or an hour. Think about things and places that can be used to evoke some of the following emotions:

Spooky

old, abandoned house	owl's cry
dark cellar	moon/no moon
thick forest	banging shutters
strange tower	dog howling
midnight	footsteps
howling wind	gust of cold wind
clanking sounds	

Cozy

fireplace	book
rag rug	sunny window
cat	marshmallows
dog	flowers/plants
hot drink	keepsake locket
warm blanket	

See how many places or props you can think of that evoke the following feelings:

happy	worried
sad	anxious
challenging	cheerful
exciting	silly
angry	

SPECIFIC VS. GENERAL

Settings are usually conveyed to the reader in enough detail to anchor the scene. By the end of the first several pages of a middle-grade or young-adult novel, the reader knows where he is and when the story is happening. Some of the details used to anchor scenes in older fiction are the following:

real place names
details of dress, vehicles, etc., revealing period
reference to historical personages/events
exotic foods
foreign words
unfamiliar ceremonies
foreign names
unusual animals/plants
actual dates
antiquated or unfamiliar diction in dialogue

The great exception to the use of such specifics is the classic fairy tales, which are deliberately set in no particular place and in no specific time. "Once upon a time" is an invitation to readers to enter into a world where time and place do not exist. The fairy-tale setting is a very useful one for a writer. The well-known stories are in the public domain, which means that a writer can rewrite them, twist them or set them in a specific place (e.g., Berthe's *The Cajun Gingerbread Boy*, set in southwestern Louisiana). Look at the mix-and-match list below and try to think of one of the classic stories in one of the unexpected settings.

Cinderella	New York City
Jack and the Beanstalk	clipper ship
Beauty and the Beast	Old West
Sleeping Beauty	Ancient Greece
Hansel and Gretel	circus caravan
Snow White and the Seven Dwarfs	contemporary China

Children's books often explore other realms and worlds: planets, fantasy worlds, foreign lands and other ages:

Prehistory	Medieval times
Stone Age	American Revolution

American West   Biblical times
Civil War

Children's books for all ages also explore other cultures. Remember that a setting looks different depending on whose eyes do the viewing. For instance, a book set in the American West would look different from the point of view of a Native American character than if seen through the eyes of a white rancher's son:

African American   European
Native American   Asian American
Hispanic

FANTASY VS. REALITY

Settings are infinite and all-important to the success of your story idea. If you are writing fantasy and it is not the fairy-tale variety, you will have to create your own world. You need a clear vision of what that world looks like, where it is, what kind of beings people it, what kinds of laws govern its nature. If you want the perfect example of a successfully created world, read Ursula K. LeGuin's *Earthsea Trilogy*. An original and convincing fantasy world is one of the most difficult things to create, and our advice is to avoid it unless you have a deep desire and clear vision of what you want. Inexperienced writers don't always realize that a fantasy world has as many "laws of nature" as the real world. Magic wands that grant every wish do not work. There is always a limitation to magic, whether it be the number of wishes the heroine can make or something else. You must determine what that limitation is and stick to it. Here are some things to consider in formulating your fantasy world:

gravity/no gravity
water/no water
air/no air
inhabitants' anatomy
special homes
special diets
dress
technology to cope with environment's peculiarities

human/nonhuman characters
family structure
other thinking creatures inhabiting world
natural/supernatural forces
language
belief system (religion or other)
advanced/primitive society
topography
vegetation
animal life
names

If, on the other hand, your setting is a place in the real world, you will have to research your setting. You will want your setting to be absolutely authentic. Be careful not to have tropical flowers blooming at the North Pole! Here are aspects to consider carefully in setting your story in a real place:

climate
flora and fauna
city and street names
language
history
geography or layout
seasonal changes
famous personages associated with place
well-known buildings
architecture
styles of housing
natural disasters

Sometimes a book may benefit from both a fantasy setting and a realistic one. In *The Wizard of Oz*, L. Frank Baum took Dorothy from a realistic Kansas to the fantastic world of Oz and back again. His Kansas reflects the plainness of the real state and exploited its proneness to tornadoes. Oz is a carefully defined world laid out in sectors dedicated to different types of creatures.

Here is an exercise that may help in the successful creation of a full world like Oz: Create a map of your new world. Indicate the four cardinal points of the compass and determine what goes in which sector of the map. As you work, think about varying the terrain. Doing so may help you vary the things and personages found in different areas, making a more varied and interesting setting. Try to stick to your plan as you work through your story. In your thinking, decide whether and where your setting has the following features:

hills	farmland
plains	cities
bodies of water	roads
woods	deserts
caves	beaches
large rocks	oases
cliffs	

Defining the setting may also be helpful in determining the nature of some of the inhabitants. For instance, Oz features trees that can grab passersby and throw them to the ground, as well as moving, talking people made of china. What special characteristics do your fantasy-world inhabitants have?

HISTORICAL SETTING

Some successful authors employ researchers to study history, flora and fauna, and the legends and culture of the place where the story is set. The result may be detail so accurate the reader can almost feel the weather, smell the plants, see the mountains.

In books for children, a historical setting is appropriate for adventure stories and, of course, biographies. It is also often the perfect setting for a contemporary theme that might be awkward or less effective if placed in a contemporary setting. Here are several historical settings that have been successfully evoked in children's books, together with some features of each one:

Prehistory (Before Man/After the Dinosaurs)

Cro-Magnon Man
Neanderthal Man

origins of fire
sea life
pterosaurs and other birdlike creatures
evolution
cave dwelling
cave painting
hunting and gathering
clothing made of animal skins
tiny mammals
woolly mammoths
saber-toothed tigers
carving
making/playing musical instruments
magnolia trees

Ancient World (Greece/Egypt/Rome)

sailing ships with oars
pyramids
temples
wall carvings
writing
archery

lyres and flutes
chariots
horses
tunics/togas
sacrifices to gods
scrolls

Medieval World (Europe)

monastery
cathedral
gargoyles
fairs
farming implements
plow
thatched hut
hose

wimple
illuminated books
sorcery
walled city
castle keep
moat
crossbow

Enlightenment (Revolutionary Era)

musket
tailcoat

powdered wig
harpsichord

songbird   rubber
exotic imported animals,   cannon
      plants, foods, fabrics   galleon
tea   broadsheet
coffee   telescope
chocolate

Nineteenth Century (Civil War and After)

quilt	drum
covered wagon	rifle
factory	revolver
plantation house	armored ship
railroad	ballot box
sun bonnet	newspaper
fife	

Twentieth Century

automobile	synthesizer
airplane	Web browser
space rocket	movies
X ray	short skirts
armored tank	phonograph
telephone	radio
computer	television

Check out the following mix-and-match list for contemporary themes that might be particularly interesting in a historical setting. Remember that the theme can be somewhat disguised to fit in with the surroundings you choose. In the play *The Crucible*, Arthur Miller wrote about McCarthy Era blacklisting but set his story in the days of the Salem witch trials. One situation was a good metaphor for the other. For children, you may have to draw the parallels a bit more explicitly than Miller did in his play.

homosexuality	Revolutionary War
substance abuse	The Crusades

single parent	The Trojan War
poverty	westward expansion
mental illness	Civil War
abuse/neglect	Russian Revolution
racism	Voyages of Discovery

Many writers of older fiction have placed their young characters in the thick of historical events. You can get started by imagining your young character in one of the following dramatic situations. Included is some basic information about the era to help you begin your research:

Building the Great Pyramid Built over a period of twenty years around 2500 B.C., the Great Pyramid was one of the finest flowerings of Ancient Egyptian civilization. There are conflicting theories as to the existence and nature of slave labor in that time, but the 100,000 workers who contributed to the erection of the structure were surely lower-caste individuals. The secret passageways inside the solid pyramid may provide interesting settings in themselves. What role might young people have played?

Children's Crusade The period of the Crusades, when European powers determined to recapture Jerusalem from the Muslims, was a time of almost unprecedented brutality throughout Europe and the Middle East. In 1212, many children left their homes throughout Europe with the purpose of helping the effort without violence. Many of the children were sold into slavery.

Voyage of Marco Polo A Venetian merchant, Marco Polo was one of the first Europeans to explore the Far East. Traveling overland in 1271, Marco viewed the rich, exotic world stretching from the Middle East to Kublai Khan's court in China. Marco and his companions did not return to Italy until 1295. Marco was in his teens when he first left on his travels.

World of the Aztecs The Aztecs developed a powerful civilization that dominated central Mexico starting about 1325. Their accomplishments included marvels of architecture (the pyramids), engineering (a capital city built on canals) and astronomy (exceptionally precise calendars). In 1521, the Spanish conquistador Cortés arrived from Spain, and the great civilization was virtually destroyed. Imagine this setting from the point of view of an Aztec youth. Now see it through the eyes of a Spanish cabin boy accompanying Cortés' expedition.

French Revolution Beginning in 1789, the revolutionary period saw the overthrow of the French monarchy and the establishment of a republican form of government. The period was marked by class struggle, rioting in the streets and mass executions of aristocrats, clergy members and others. Again, shifting perspectives suggest different interesting facets of this experience: a young aristocrat would see the scene differently from a young pauper.

Battle of Bull Run/Battle of Manassas In 1861, at the start of the Civil War, The First Battle of Bull Run, or the Battle of Manassas as it is called in the South, was the first major military engagement between North and South. Union holiday-makers, certain of victory due to the greater number of their troops, accompanied the army from Washington, DC. However, the Union troops were put to flight, in large part due to the actions of Confederate Gen. Stonewall Jackson. This battle was the first suggestion that the war would be a long and bloody one. The perspective of a young recruit or sightseer might be interesting.

Freedom march During the Civil Rights Movement of the 1960s, Selma, Alabama, was the scene of a campaign to register Black voters led by the Reverend Dr. Martin Luther King, Jr. There was violent opposition to this campaign, and Dr. King organized a march from Selma to the state capital at Montgomery. Many children and young people were part of the march, and their early exposure to racism and violence provide a fascinating perspective on this moment in history.

In choosing a historical setting, you commit yourself to doing lots of research to guarantee the accuracy of your set-dressing. Also consider what the lives of children and young people were like in those times. Issues of social station and affluence will be important factors in answering the following questions:

- Did they go to school?
- Did they work?
- Did they live with their families?
- Were they apprenticed to craftsmen?

- Could they change occupations?
- Could they choose their own mates?
- Did they travel?
- Did they read and write?
- What kind of health care did they have?
- What did they do for fun?

The advantage of a contemporary setting is that your theme or idea might be more accessible in a milieu familiar to the reader. By that we mean that if you're writing about divorce and its effect on children, the problems are contemporary and can be brought out clearly in the story. However, a more subtle approach to the same theme might be a tale set in another century and showing how difficult it is for a child to have parents who are separated. As an example, you might develop the story of Mary Tudor, daughter of King Henry VIII and Catherine of Aragon. Mary's father was so determined to divorce her mother that he changed his country's religion and executed some of his closest and most loyal advisers. The teenaged Mary was forced to separate from her mother, to whom she was very close. In addition to the changes in her family environment, Mary's succession rights and thus her career prospects were thrown into doubt. Surely many poignant issues about divorce could be illustrated in a well-researched historical YA novel about Mary Tudor. However, although Mary's feelings about her family situation would resonate today, you would waste much of the value of the distinctive setting if you failed to provide an accurate depiction of Mary's Renaissance world.

In a book on divorce for younger readers, you might want to use animal characters so the child reader can distance himself from the emotional reality of his situation but at the same time empathize with the characters. *Dinosaurs Divorce* by Laurene Krasny Brown and Marc Brown is a picture book that takes this approach.

"DATED" TOPICS

The danger of a contemporary setting that focuses on a specific problem is that it might date your book. Although it might answer a burning question of the moment, the answer might not be relevant to a different age. This is particularly true of problem-solving young adult novels. For example, in a bookstore about five years ago, a woman came in and asked for a "book on divorce." The bookseller gave her a title that had just been published. That book is no longer in print—it was too specifically contemporary and suggested solutions no longer recommended by child psychologists.

Examples of dated settings no longer relevant for young children abound. For example, an editor was not interested in a book that showed a child how to tie a shoelace even though the story was cleverly told in words and pictures. The creator had forgotten that most shoes for very young children have Velcro closures! If you choose a contemporary setting, research it carefully and be aware of the many changes that have taken place in the child's world today. Take note of some of the following contemporary variants on things children need or enjoy:

Then	Now
shoelace	Velcro
watch	digital watch
phonograph	portable CD player
typewriter	computer
notes	E-mail
telephone	cell phone
party dress	wide bell-bottoms and T-shirt
Beatles	Hanson
high heels	chunky heels

Of course, a good story transcends time. Eleanor Estes' *The Hundred Dresses* is a classic despite the fact that now a more contemporary title might be *The Hundred Pairs of Jeans.* The most important function of your setting is to provide a consistent, thematically relevant context for your characters and their actions.

The very best in children's books are as valid today as they were when they were written, but in all but those very few, you can find clues that pinpoint the publication date. You will see that the setting usually reveals the social mores of the time. Victorian books exhibit a "children should be seen and not heard" morality. Choose your setting carefully and make sure that it accomplishes what you want of it without "dating" it. Books written in the sixties express very liberal views. If you feel uncomfortable using a contemporary setting, here are ways to familiarize yourself with whatever is *au courant* for the age you intend to write for.

Ways to Make You "Literate" in Contemporary Settings:

- Visit a playground (famous folklorists collected their rhymes this way)
- Sit in on a classroom
- Eavesdrop at a coffee shop that caters to teenagers (a very well-known YA author does this!)
- Read YAs, chapter books and picture books
- Watch TV programs designed for the age group you intend to write for
- Surf the Internet (try not to get lost in the myriad possibilities of contemporary settings and situations you'll encounter!)

AMBIANCE

Atmosphere or ambiance is part of setting, sometimes the most important part. Think of Edgar Allan Poe's "The Fall of the House of Usher" or any other ghost story. The atmosphere can be used to set the scene and put the reader in the right frame of mind.

Madeleine L'Engle's *A Wrinkle in Time* begins as follows:

> It was a dark and stormy night.
>
> In her attic room Margaret Murry, wrapped in an old patchwork quilt, sat on the foot of her bed and watched the trees tossing in the frenzied lashing of the wind. Every few moments the moon ripped through them, creating wraith-like shadows along the ground.
>
> The house was dark.
>
> Wrapped in her quilt, Meg shook.

The reader shakes a bit, too! The setting has set the stage for a dramatic, suspenseful tale: a setting that prepares the way for a perfect blend of realism and fantasy. You can create such a vivid setting, too, if you will use your five senses to describe the scene in your mind's eye. Consider the following sensations and use your impressions to describe place, weather and things to set the mood:

Sight

color	size
brightness	focus
closeness	shape

Sound

volume	source
harshness	direction
distance	

Smell

freshness	spiciness
foulness	faintness
sweetness	strength
smokiness	

Touch

| smoothness | coarseness |
| temperature | bumpiness |

Taste

salt	temperature
sweet	smoothness
bitter	crunchiness

In *Goodnight Moon,* the setting is bedtime in a child's room as darkness approaches. The atmosphere of warmth and comfort is wonderfully established. There is no formula for creating such a classic. But clues to *Goodnight Moon*'s lasting popularity emerge when you analyze the setting. Indeed, the book is almost all setting. Colors are an important theme in the story. The book takes place in one room, and by the end of the story the reader knows the room intimately. You should be as painstaking with the setting of your own story. In the text, Margaret Wise Brown describes:

bed	sky
chair	air
table	child
toys	food
books	dishes
clothes	

Goodnight Moon tells us how all-important setting is in picture books for the youngest child. Here are some suggested settings:

Situation as Setting	Place and Home	Time
a baby-sitter arrives	a well-known room	end of day
parents go out	grandmother's house	beginning of day
first fishing experience	a lake	mealtime
first time	the zoo	weekend
	the beach	vacation
	at the sea	summertime
	the garden	springtime
	the woods	autumn
	day care	nursery-school time
	on a farm	Christmastime

RESEARCH

Read books in the genre you are writing and pay attention to the settings. Is it right for the story? Just because it's in print doesn't make it the best. Can you think of a better setting to showcase the characters and plot problems?

As you research your book, jot down details you might want to use. When you think your setting is a vague or empty place, refer to your notes and "decorate" your setting.

Books with fantasy-world settings worth studying:

Aesop's Fables—These stories are set in a timeless world where animals talk.

Gulliver's Travels by Jonathan Swift—This classic features four different worlds, most famously Lilliput, the land of tiny people; each domain is thoroughly imagined and evoked.

"The Legend of Sleepy Hollow" by Washington Irving—The setting of this story is realistic New York State during the days of Dutch settlement. The author makes the weird events recounted in the story convincing in this background.

Alice in Wonderland by Lewis Carroll—Wonderland is a fantasy world "down the rabbit hole," where Alice meets animals that dress and talk like Victorian adults, playing cards with arms and legs, etc. The world has a dreamlike logic all its own.

At the Back of the North Wind by George MacDonald—The story is set in realistic London until the young hero visits the land "at the back of the north wind, a lush bucolic land."

Pinocchio by Carlo Collodi—This book's world looks similar to the world around us except that some animals and inanimate objects can walk and talk like people do. There is an element of magic in Pinocchio's world, introduced principally by the Blue Child.

The Enchanted Castle by E. Nesbit—The castle appears realistic until the children find that wishes made there actually become reality.

The Wizard of Oz by L. Frank Baum—This book includes several fantastic realms, including the Land of the Munchkins and the Emerald City, all fully imagined and described in detail.

The Tale of Peter Rabbit by Beatrix Potter—Peter and his family inhabit a realistic rustic world of woods and farms, except the animals dress and converse as if they were human.

Peter Pan by James M. Barrie—Beginning in Edwardian London, the characters eventually arrive in Never Land, where all children's favorite fantasies—pirates, Indians, no adults—come alive.

The Wind in the Willows by Kenneth Grahame—Though an accurate depiction of English country life, the book is populated by animals in human clothing. The characters' occasional interactions with actual humans are anything but realistic. There is basically no magic in the book.

The Story of Dr. Dolittle by Hugh Lofting—The doctor's story begins in the realistic English village of Puddleby. Dr. Dolittle has the exceptional ability to talk to animals in their own language. His travels eventually land him in a comical and completely unrealistic African kingdom.

Winnie-the-Pooh by A.A. Milne—The world of these stories is the play world of a child's imagining. If his stuffed toys were living animals, surely they would live in the hollow trees and burrows of Christopher Robin's make-believe world.

Mary Poppins by P.L. Travers—The children's world is a prosaic upper-crust British one. However, the stern and matter-of-fact Mary Poppins brings magic in her wake, much as she denies it. The magic comes not through the setting but through a character (or, actually, though the children's perceptions).

Here is a list of classics dependent on a geographical or historical setting:

The Story of Ferdinand by Munro Leaf (cork groves and bull rings of Spain)

Madeline by Ludwig Bemelmans (Parisian orphanage)

A Christmas Carol by Charles Dickens (nineteenth-century London)

Zlateh the Goat by Isaac Bashevis Singer (Eastern European shtetl)

Little Women by Louisa May Alcott (Civil War-era New England)

Caddie Woodlawn by Carol Ryrie Brink (frontier days in Wisconsin)

War Comes to Willy Freeman by James Lincoln Collier and Christopher Collier (African-American life in the Revolutionary Era)

The Courage of Sarah Noble by Alice Dalgliesh (wilderness in Colonial America)

Columbus by Ingri and Edgar Parin d'Aulaire (Genoa to Spain to America in the fifteenth century)

The Door in the Wall by Marguerite de Angeli (thirteenth-century England)

The House of Sixty Fathers by Meindert de Jong (Japanese-occupied China)

Johnny Tremain by Esther Forbes (Revolutionary Massachusetts)

The Slave Dancer by Paula Fox (1840 slave ship)

The Diary of a Young Girl by Anne Frank (Nazi-occupied Amsterdam)

And Then What Happened, Paul Revere? by Jean Fritz (Revolutionary Boston)

Across Five Aprils by Irene Hunt (Civil War in the border states)

The Walking Stones by Mollie Hunter (old-time Scotland)

When Hitler Stole Pink Rabbit by Judith Kerr (World War II Europe)

Sarah, Plain and Tall by Patricia MacLachlan (Western frontier)

Island of the Blue Dolphins by Scott O'Dell (West Coast, early nineteenth century)

The Witch of Blackbird Pond by Elizabeth George Speare (early Colonial Connecticut)

Little House on the Prairie by Laura Ingalls Wilder (frontier Midwest)

Here is a list of successful books using contemporary settings in problem-solving young adult novels:

The Chocolate War by Robert Cormier (all-boys Catholic high school)

Representing Super Doll by Richard Peck (New York beauty pageant)

Are You There God? It's Me, Margaret by Judy Blume (mixed-religion home)

Forever by Judy Blume (high school)

Dinky Hocker Shoots Smack by M.E. Kerr (Weight Watchers)

A Hero Ain't Nothin' But a Sandwich by Alice Childress (inner city)

I Am the Cheese by Robert Cormier (bicycle trip)

The Outsiders by S.E. Hinton (gang warfare)

Holes by Louis Sachar (summer camp)

Gulf by Robert Westall (Persian Gulf War)

Sun Dance by Kevin McColley (road trip)

A hybrid that poses particular challenges for setting is the time-warp story. In this type of work, a character is transported from one time and place to another. Margaret Murry in Madeleine L'Engle's *A Wrinkle in Time* is a good example, as she is transported from her realistic modern American home to a faraway, futuristic planet where her father is held hostage. In a book of this nature, you must double your work. You will need two settings, each credible, and a believable bridge between the two worlds. Eleanor Cameron's *The Court of the Stone Children* is a good example. In picture books, look at Maurice Sendak's *Outside Over There*, where the heroine's quest takes her to a fairy world.

Be sure your setting is as good as it gets—detailed and believable. If it's just good, it should and can be better.

Chapter Six

Plot

Plot is probably the most essential ingredient in a book you can't put down or one your child begs to have read over and over, or if he's older, a book he reads with a flashlight after lights are out and he's supposed to be asleep. It's that feeling of "I've got to know what happens next" that makes the reader turn a page.

In books for younger children, plot is easy to see—it is the something different that happens on each page. You have thirty-two pages in a picture book, and that usually means approximately twenty-five or so incidents comprising the plot of the book. Your plot outline is really your book dummy, where you draw or describe the picture on each page. For a picture-book plot to work, something different must happen in each picture. But that something needn't be very different—a dramatic change in a character's facial expression may be sufficient in some instances. Here are some of the changes that can drive the next incident in your picture book:

    change of scene
    entrance or exit of character
    change of expression
    close-up
    panorama
    change of point of view
    change of mood
    surprise
    more of the same
    meanwhile . . . (what's happening elsewhere)

Logic and cause-and-effect are two of the most important things picture books teach. Your plot—the transitions from picture to picture and from page to page—must be logical, sequential, motivated by the main character's actions (if you are writing fiction) and related to illustrating the strong theme of your book. If you find yourself using sophisticated narrative techniques like flashbacks, rethink your plot. A picture book should almost always take place in one time frame and move in a direct line from start to finish.

BEGIN AT THE BEGINNING

The beginning is a problem area for many picture-book writers. Always start where the story becomes interesting. Many writers begin with background, character introductions, etc. Eliminate the preliminaries. You don't have room for them in a picture book. Start where the story becomes interesting and grab the reader's attention right away. Here are some signs to help you identify your beginning:

dramatic piece of dialogue

first experience of strong emotion

character makes a decision

day begins

introduce character's present situation

character's typical response to specific situation, which may change or be reinforced in story ("Timmy always liked to . . .")

beginning of a journey

character receives or sends an important message

The classic fairy tales offer good examples of how to start where the characters' problem is. You should do the same—begin where the character is experiencing or about to experience the crisis that will determine his actions. Here are some examples from the Brothers Grimm:

no more money and no way to get any

husband and wife want a child but can't have one

character's hopes (as for inheritance) are disappointed

character is forced to leave home

character is born with unusual physical quality
character returns home from journey/adventure/war
character encounters mysterious/magical stranger
character hears of opportunity to improve his lot
character receives special/magical gift

WHAT DRIVES PLOT?

Format

In storybooks, easy-to-read books and chapter books, your plot or plots will not be so closely linked with the book's format. The pictures will be more incidental, so you must make sure your plot is internally logical and motivated. The best way to do so, as in any book, is to create a strong, consistent character who drives the action forward. A good example from the easy-to-read world is Peggy Parish's Amelia Bedelia. Amelia interprets common turns of phrase literally, and in this she is very much like a child learning to read. When Amelia, a maid, is instructed to "draw the curtains," she takes a pencil and pad and makes a picture of the curtains. Her consistent but well-intentioned misunderstandings make the stories happen.

Characterization

In books for older readers, character is also paramount in determining the plot, what happens in the story. But when you analyze page-turners, and you should if you are writing a book for children, you realize you care about what happens next because you are involved with the main character and wonder how he or she will handle a particular situation. The story interests you because you know him, his plight, his choices, his good traits and bad, and you are curious about how, in this particular setting, he'll proceed. *Curious* and *main character* are the key words.

You wouldn't be curious about plot if the main character had a blank face and was not "real" in your mind, or if the setting or situation he's in weren't interesting. It wouldn't matter to you whether he sank or swam or where his situation placed him or how he proceeded. Plot is cause and effect and is dependent on characterization and setting.

A perfect example of what we mean comes straight from the pages of Louisa May Alcott's *Little Women*. The impoverished March family is worried about Father, who is ill at the front during the Civil War. Ever one to take action, Jo goes to a wig-maker and sells her long auburn hair, her one physical beauty, in order to get some extra money to send for Father's care. This action is motivated by love, devotion, generosity and a certain impulsiveness. After returning home and bravely explaining her action, the following scene ensues:

> Jo lay motionless, and her sister fancied that she was asleep, till a stifled sob made her exclaim, as she touched a wet cheek:
> "Jo, dear, what is it? Are you crying about Father?"
> "No, not now."
> "What then?"
> "My—my hair!" burst out poor Jo, trying vainly to smother her emotion in the pillow.

Jo's feelings drive the book's action. Her devoted act of sacrifice is certainly admirable and true to her character. But the "warts and all" depiction of her wounded vanity is what makes her real, what makes readers love her, and what makes them yearn to find out what she will do next. How will her pride influence her actions and the book's action after this point? Does this emotion have a positive side as well?

Here are some real qualities that young and old characters may have that can drive the events of an interesting plot:

proud	smug
angry	insecure
tired	impressionable
haughty	jealous
foolish	fearful
immature	foolhardy
introverted	shy
charitable	brazen

| tough | mean |
| cowardly | |

Now try to put some character traits together with some types of actions. As in the scene from *Little Women*, the tension between an outward action and an inner feeling can take your character and your plot through some interesting developments.

Emotion	Action
angry	self-sacrifice
moody	success
brave	surrender
cowardly	take a stand
loving	abandonment
secure	flee
jealous	befriend
friendly	ostracize
shy	orate
brazen	hesitate

Setting

Setting, of course, will also drive your plot. If there were no war and no faraway Father, Jo would not have to sell her hair, no matter what her personal qualities. You need a combination of character, setting and action to make the plot move. This complex is needed in even the simplest books. Let's say you are writing a board book for infants. You have your character, an infant; and your setting, baby's room. Now what makes the plot happen? Is the baby curious about his surroundings? How can a baby express this feeling?

see	wriggle
touch	flop
smell	stare
taste	sit
hear	coo
crawl	gurgle

Naturally a baby in his bedroom can do all these things. But you, the author, must put them in some kind of order. Your story needs a beginning, middle and end. In a book for infants, the beginning is often waking up in the morning. Infants thrive on a structured day, and a successful book for this audience can reflect that structure:

waking up	eating
being dressed	being washed
playing	going to sleep
taking a nap	

But a book reflecting baby's day can start in other ways, too. Think of these beginnings:

a visitor comes
Mommy leaves baby alone in the room
baby is given a new toy
time for meal/bath/nap/bed
lights out

Keep in mind that the events are only the skeleton of your story. Your story is about something else—a feeling, an experience or a theme that is special in some way. Simple events of baby's day can illustrate any of the following themes, or even others:

daddy/mommy loves me	I'm happy/sad/mad
I'm a big boy/girl	using the imagination
learning about the world	I'm well-behaved/naughty
sharing	peekaboo
playing with others	

There are other "natural" plots to give structure to your story for young children:

through the day
through the year (seasons/holidays)
dramatic part of day (bedtime, supper time)
trip to town
getting lost/getting found
wanting something/getting it
fighting/making up

animals on the farm
alphabet
numbers
misbehaving/being good

A good example of a simple board book with a plot linked to its theme is Cyndy Szekeres' *Hugs*. Each page shows a fuzzy little animal getting a hug from someone special in his world. The first plot element giving the story order and direction, then, is people in the child's world—mommy, daddy, grandpa, etc. However, the pictures also show places and times in a small child's day, so the natural progression at the end leads us from storytime to mealtime, getting undressed to bedtime. The book is *about* hugs, but the plot is provided by common occurrences in baby's day.

Once you have your beginning and the primary emotion motivating your character, something has to happen next. A curious baby wakes up. Now what does he do? It is important to develop your ability to observe the way real people behave. There are dozens of books about curious babies. What will make yours different? What will make your baby do something interesting and new, making him do something a real baby would do?

Berthe faced this issue in writing her second book, *Tom in the Middle*. The story is about the plight of the middle child who has a bossy big brother and a pesky little brother. In the first version, when Tom ran away from his brothers, Berthe said he did so "pulling his little red wagon."

"That's not what he'd really do, is it?" asked Berthe's editor.

"No, it's not," Berthe replied, thinking of her own son Tom. "He'd put on his beloved, outgrown policeman suit and he'd go to his secret place in the yard."

The feeling of truth that pervades the episode as it was finally published helps make the book much stronger. Think about some of these things that real children do as motors to drive your plot:

hide	fall down
change clothes	run away
lie	wander

| make things | watch others |
| draw | emulate older children/adults |

The plot of a book can also take place in a fantasy place of wish fulfillment. Think of some of the things kids wish for and imagine what would happen if some of those wishes came true.

dog	trip
dinosaur	airplane
pony	travel
join the circus	friend
fly	grow up
be a pirate	go to school
bicycle	live alone
car	

Again, think about different actions that can make the wish come alive and illustrate what its fulfillment could really be like. Think of the genius in Hans Christian Andersen's story "The Little Fir Tree." The story's point of departure, well disguised, is a child's wish to grow up. The events of the plot are provided by a realistic depiction of the life cycle of a Christmas tree, from sapling to firewood. The story gains poignancy from the tree's childlike wish to get bigger and see the big world. See if you can find a good plot to complement the wish your character wants fulfilled:

Wish	Action
parent's love	write letter
happy family	travel to far-off planet
acceptance of peers	draw pictures
start school	run away
live alone	make a hiding place
pet	throw a tantrum

The middle of the story should begin winding toward the conclusion as the child strives to solve the problem he's been facing all along. If it's a baby who's dropped a favorite toy out of the crib, perhaps he flops over the side (safely, of course). If it's a preteen who wants to ask out a pretty girl, perhaps he overcomes his shyness to try out for the school play of which she is the star. The most important thing in the plot of a children's book is that the solution to the plot's problem must come from the child. If the solution comes from an adult, the story will be far less satisfying to young readers and will also withhold from them the satisfaction of knowing they can solve their own problems. Of course, wise older characters, such as teachers, parents and spiritual guides, can be helpful. But the child must take action on her own to bring about the conclusion. Some of the following actions are ways a young character can take charge of the problem:

> learn something new
> tell the truth
> return home
> go to bed
> walk the dog
> enjoy/benefit from dreaded experience
> make a friend
> describe an experience
> wake up
> find what was lost

Recognize that your "child" character may sometimes be in disguise. The child character may be an adult with some childlike quality or an animal. Children will see through the mask if your character is well-developed and consistent. Amelia Bedelia, in Peggy Parish's easy-to-read series, is the child character in her stories because she interprets common idioms in a child's literal manner. Curious George is the child character in H.A. Rey's stories because he has a child's propensity for letting his natural curiosity draw him into trouble.

Once the character begins solving the problem, the story must have a climax. This is the most exciting part of your story, the part with maximum suspense because the reader is not sure the character will be able to do it. Let's say it's a toddler's board book. Your hero has been building a block tower that's getting taller and taller (the blocks' colors and shapes, or the number of blocks, can be additional plot structuring devices and also add value to your book). He's just about to crown his achievement when—*no more blocks!* This is the climax of the story. Another possible climax—the dog runs into the room and knocks over the tower.

How does it end? Perhaps he places his sippy cup on top to make up for his missing block. This, then, is a story about being inventive. If the dog knocks over the blocks and the happy baby decides to rebuild, it becomes a book about persistence. How you end the story makes all the difference, but one thing must be consistent—the ending must come from within your child character.

We want you to realize how important a well-developed character is, and how interrelated character, setting and plot are. If you haven't developed your character well enough to know how he will act, reread chapter four because a wonderful setting and an exciting plot are not enough without strong character. If you haven't placed your character in a well-researched, fascinating setting, then look at the myriad possibilities in chapter five. Make your character alive to you and your reader, place him in an interesting situation and your plotting will almost unfold by itself. At the heart of plotting is an interesting character with obstacles in his path toward his goal. Mix and match these characters and settings, and see what plot ideas come to you:

orphan	den of thieves
runaway	pirate ship
fairy child	London
illegal alien	playground
space-alien teen	fire station
migrant worker	private school
child actor	airplane
stepsibling	duck pond
teen parent	detention center
sports hero	rehabilitation center

Chances are that if your character is alive for you, he'll tell you what he's going to do. He'll tell you what he's thinking about and how he intends to act in his given situation. That is basic plot and that is what we mean by saying that the plotting will almost take care of itself.

In the last chapter, we told you how setting influences plot, how your character may act one way in a certain situation or setting and go in the opposite direction given another setting. Those three depend on each other: character, setting, plot.

To illustrate our point, think of Pocahontas, both in the many juvenile books about the historical figure and in the Walt Disney cartoon. Her crossing racial and national lines in love might be perfectly ordinary in today's culture. In the film, there's the heroine with a face like a Hollywood starlet saying things that would never have been thought in those times and using a contemporary vocabulary. Be careful of this in your writing. If you choose a period setting, these limitations on your choices may make your plot easier by reducing the possible scope of your character's actions. Think about the following factors and how your character reacts to them in her time and place:

roles of the sexes
use of profanity
slang
church-going
homogeneity/heterogeneity of community
means of travel
proximity to other places
schooling
class structure
rural vs. urban setting
child labor
existing technology
natural resources
wartime/peacetime
political structure
wealth vs. poverty

If you are writing a picture book, you can do a simple plot breakdown by making your own book dummy and deciding what the picture will show on each page or spread. As you can see from the example of the baby and the blocks, a simple change in the plot may result in an entirely different story.

If you are writing a longer book, you should begin with an outline. A good rule of thumb is: Make your plot outline and know where you're going before you start. Think of your outline as a road map. Here's an example: A family is traveling from New Orleans to New York. They will go by car for the father's all-important job interview, and the family will not be returning no matter the outcome of the interview. He has quit his New Orleans job, pulled the children out of school, etc. Middle: It is a three-day trip and he loses a day because the car breaks down. The children know their father is erratic, but his lack of advance planning really makes them worry. He is in danger of missing the interview, and the children may miss the start of the school year. More problems occur en route. A stranger delays them. Everything else that could happen to delay them does. Tension mounts. Unexpected things threaten the whole plan—then one of the children is kidnapped! Somewhere in the middle you have planted a "hook" that will ultimately influence your solution.

Endings

1. **The child is easily found.** The family arrives on time and the father has a successful interview and gets the job. (This structure does not work because there is no plot without problems.)

2. **The child is rescued.** Against all odds, the father arrives on time, having successfully surmounted his problems en route and gets the job! (This structure does not work because it is too predictable.)

3. **The child cannot be found.** Having turned matters over to the police, the father and the embittered other child arrive late. The father misses the interview and all of his bridges are seemingly burned, until the stranger he met on the road turns out to be a savior or until . . . fill in with your idea.

The end need not be set in stone when you start writing. For that matter, neither is the middle. If you have your skeleton plot, you can flesh it out as you write. There used to be a successful genre of middle-grade books that allowed the reader to "choose his own adventure."

These intricately plotted books contained several versions of the same story. At crucial moments in the story, the reader was prompted to turn to one page if he wanted the plot to take one turn, to another page if he wanted a different outcome. "Choose your own adventure" can be a good exercise if you're not sure where your story is going. Try the different choices and see which one feels right. In the middle of the story, your character can:

take a different direction
make a decision
change clothes
hop aboard a conveyance
change his behavior
feel a new emotion
act out of character (if for a reason clear to the reader)
help/ignore one in need
ask a question

At the end, your character can:
reach the goal
fail to reach the goal
learn an important lesson
teach others an important lesson
learn to change his behavior
forgive a loved one
strike out on his own
make a friend

The trick is to lay out your journey in outline form from beginning to end. But you, the author, are free to alter your route, even your destination. If you give your creative mind freedom and if you have developed your characters fully in an interesting setting, those characters and the choices they encounter will guide your plot and suggest exciting alternate routes to your final destination.

As you plot along (pun intended) always ask yourself: Is this the way my character would really behave given the circumstances? Never, ever make your character act to convenience your prearranged plot! Ask yourself: Is this the most intriguing way I should go? What are some alternative, more original routes? Look at the following factors:

- What's she wearing?
- Where is she going?
- To whom is she talking?
- What are her choices?
- How will she get there?
- When will she arrive?
- What should she say?
- What does she say?
- What does she want?
- What does she think she wants?
- How could she do this differently?

Remember that life is truly stranger than fiction and the unexpected is more exciting than the predictable. It can happen in your story. But make it happen to the plot, not to the character (e.g., no unexplained conversions, no miraculous cures or fantastic coincidences). We can think of many books that are unsuccessful because the ending was forced.

THEME

The theme holding your plot together need not be new. In fact, there are no new themes. There will always be love and hate, loneliness and greed, coming of age, all of the seven deadly sins and all of the beatitudes that have already been used. The classic themes for children's and young-adult books are:

family	the world around you
learning	nature
being yourself	feelings
growing up	making friends
using imagination	sharing
taking responsibility	new experiences
pets/animals	

These themes are not new. How they are used is yours, and that is plot. That is where your originality and your creative talent can shine and make your book different, worthwhile and a page-turner for children.

Plotting your book should take place in your mind at the beginning when you first have your idea. Do some "stream-of-consciousness" thinking, that is, think about your idea and let it roam. Take notes if you're afraid you'll forget your thoughts before you have a chance to start your "real" writing. Then write down the bare bones of your outline, and, to use another metaphor, hang your notes on the "skeleton outline" of:

I. Beginning
II. Middle
III. End

Start writing soon. You'll be surprised at how fast the words will flow. Don't forget—you are not writing in cement and part or all can be thrown out. You may want to write a scene that takes place in the middle of the book first, the one that excites you the most. Go ahead and do it. It may turn out to be the best part of your writing or it may have to be tossed out when you finally get your book written. Throwing out a good scene is difficult to do, but don't force the fit. In the end, your plot must move along seamlessly and relentlessly, but eliminate scenes at the end of the writing process rather than being intimidated by your outline and not writing what appears to be an unnecessary scene.

When writing a young-adult novel (ages ten and up) or any chapter book (ages six to ten), your plot will be far more complex than the plot of a picture book (ages one to six). This unfortunately does not make the picture book easier to write or plot. It's more difficult to say something meaningful in a few words than in several paragraphs in which you can explain and clarify. Try writing a haiku or a poem if you want to prove that to yourself. Study some of the classic picture books to see how few words are used. Think of a theme like loneliness or love, and write a succinct sentence that expresses the emotion.

Study the plots in classic picture books:

Millions of Cats by Wanda Gag—A man sets out to find a cat to cure his wife's loneliness, and the scrawniest one of millions develops into the ideal pet.

Where the Wild Things Are by Maurice Sendak—A little boy is punished for his misbehavior and conquers his resultant fearful emotions.

The Tale of Peter Rabbit by Beatrix Potter—A naughty bunny is almost baked into a pie but escapes from Farmer MacGregor and gets back to his family.

The Story of Babar by Jean de Brunhoff—A little elephant encounters human civilization, then returns as an elegant king to his jungle home.

Sylvester and the Magic Pebble by William Steig—A young donkey finds a wishing pebble and accidentally turns himself into a rock but finally changes back.

Mirette on the High Wire by Emily Arnold McCully—A little girl becomes determined to learn to walk on the high-wire from a retired circus artist.

Officer Buckle and Gloria by Peggy Rathmann—A policeman and his dog love to give safety talks at schools, until the officer decides the students like his dog best.

There are no new ideas or themes in books about naughty boys and rabbits or loneliness and wanting a pet. It's the plot, the way the author handles the story line, that makes each of these stories original and a classic. You can do it, too. As we have suggested before, take your idea and plot it in the form of:

I. Beginning
II. Middle
III. Ending

Now start writing and get it all down, changing directions if necessary. When you're through and your skeleton is fleshed out, put it on a diet and get rid of excess fat: those digressions, hackneyed adjectives, clichés, etc.—everything that doesn't move your plot along.

If you think of plot as problem-solving, the horizon widens considerably for older children who are ready to start school or are already in school. Ages four to eight are wonderful audiences for writers. These children are curious about the world outside the home. Everything is new; everything is interesting. Children of this age are like dry sponges soaking in the experiences of each new day. Suddenly there are more people involved in their lives: other children, teachers and new authority figures, extended families, storekeepers. Each day brings a new situation, a widening of the child's world.

Now we are ready for simple plotting. We have our characters and our setting or situation and our characters react to their setting or situation. How they do this is basic plot.

In the picture book *Goodnight Moon* by Margaret Wise Brown, a child says good night to everything in his room. But something more would have to follow for an older child.

Then what? In a book for older children, there might be a monster hiding under his bed and he cannot fall asleep until he's conquered it. Instead of just one step, saying good night to everything, there is the obstacle, or step 2, the imaginary monster under the bed, which necessitates step 3, conquering the monster so that sleep comes. Books for this age group need a beginning, a middle and an end; they need a plot, not just a setting of atmosphere or place.

Something has to happen or you'll lose your young reader in a hurry. Children do not read books that bore them. That means your plot should fascinate them. Your book has a lot of competition from other books, toys, television and electronic games. Your book has to be sensational. The obstacle that confronts the hero or heroine should be an exciting one that doesn't have a predictable ending.

Beware, too, of the disguised sermon. A book for children should teach and carry a message, which we call the theme, but it should be interwoven into a seamless, intriguing plot. Story is always paramount in a successful book for children.

It sounds simplistic and repetitive to say that plots have a beginning, a middle and an end, but the middle, which consists of the necessary problem or obstacle, is what gives your book a plot and makes it into a complete story.

Look at plot this way: You write a story about a child who goes on a picnic. You describe the excited child waking up, the preparations, the car trip, the food served, the games played, the trip home, the tired child going to bed. You describe everything in great detail but there is no plot unless there is a problem solved or some change takes place. Something has to happen to change things. Again, character may be the key. In a book for young children, it may be sufficient that the child character doesn't want to leave the picnic and go home, or that he was too little to take part in the sack race. For a young adult, it could be that his love interest never showed up.

Here is a true-life story:

Two eight-year-old boys are having a birthday-football party in the park. All twenty of the boys in their class are invited. There is a big table set with the cake, and there is an ice chest with ice cream and cold drinks. Both boys and their parents are waiting for the guests. Just before the guests arrives, one boy's dad throws his son a football and the boy, trying to catch the pass, slips in the mud and breaks his arm. When he returns to the party from the hospital with his arm in a cast, the last guest has left and the party is over. This is a true story but it has no plot. It is the description of sequential events. To make it into a plotted story, the boy had to do something because he broke his arm.

Taking a set of events from real life is not enough to make a good story. However, those events can suggest different endings. Keep in mind that truth is not only stranger than fiction but is more difficult to convert into fiction. There has to be cause and effect to make plot. Your character and theme will be crucial in turning the events into a coherent plot that illustrates an idea. Here are a few suggested endings. See if you can come up with others.

- The guests have decided to move the party to the boy's house and surprise him when he gets home. (Theme: Friends are thoughtful.)
- The disappointed boy goes home, and his little brother, whom he excluded from the party as being too little, helps him celebrate his birthday. (Theme: Be nice to your little brother.)
- The boy, having arrived back at the park, is disappointed that the guests are gone; but his favorite football hero is walking the dog and signs his cast. (Theme: Every cloud has a silver lining.)

Remember that how you develop events will affect your beginning, too. If you were to develop the "little brother" version of the plot, you would begin the story not at the park but at home when the protagonist bars his little brother from the party. In the "football hero" plot, you would have to introduce the protagonist's admiration for the hero early in the book.

PLOT AND AGE GROUP

In a plotted story, your main character follows a course of action by overcoming obstacles to reach a predetermined goal.

Plots are so simple for the youngest child that they are barely plots. Here are some:

Learning Basic Skills

alphabet	colors
numbers	dressing
shapes	food
textures	

Understanding Roles

mother	siblings
father	self

Performing Tasks

eating	sleeping
playing	

Recognizing Objects

animals	words
household items	

Information About

animals	world around you
flowers	

Simple Formats

touch-and-feel books	simple jigsaw-puzzle books
lift-the-flap books	

Another plot type for youngest children is the cumulative story. The perfect examples are the rhymes "The House That Jack Built" and "The Farmer in the Dell." Basically, each episode involves the addition of one object to the scene. The toddler's building-block story mentioned earlier in this chapter is a simple original example.

In picture books, the illustrations always contain elements of plot. In wordless books for the youngest, plots are carried entirely in the illustrations. The illustrations must be clear and the objects pictured recognizable. You may choose to "write" a wordless book where you know the action will be crystal clear from the pictures. Generally, stories focused on subtle shifts of emotion are not suited for wordless treatment. Think of these books as the silent movies of picture books and make sure the plot is action-oriented. Here are some plot ideas that may be very clear in pictures without words:

getting lost	catching up with the others
walking through woods	following siblings to school
being chased by an animal	playing in a rhythm band
climbing a tree	dancing
jumping off a rock	eating
dressing up	hugging

The youngest "reader" does not understand time. Tomorrow means "not now" or "never" to her, and so most picture-book plots for the very youngest are acted out in a single event:

playtime	getting dressed
bath time	outing
supper time	waking
bedtime	meeting others

getting a present	cuddling
building	making noise
swinging	

Children four to six years old are dramatically more knowledge-able and have mastered an amazing number of skills. These readers are ready for stories with plots, but because of the picture-book format, there are very few words and each one counts. Keep the plot simple. A simple idea is sufficient. As in any book, there is still a need for conflict, but the scale or difficulty may be less than in books for older readers. Here is a mix-and-match list of settings and obstacles for books in this age range:

picnic	insects
play date	illness
beach	storm
farm	nurturing pet
starting school	broken leg
birthday party	too little
Christmas	bedtime
new home	flat tire

Books for children eight to ten are perhaps the most fertile field for plotting. Children are still unaffectedly enthusiastic about the world around them and are ready for complex stories with difficult obstacles and not always "they lived happily ever after" endings. The one rule here is that the ending should not be hopeless. A book for children should always show that there are ways out of difficulties even if the ending is sad.

Remember that the two most difficult subjects to deal with are God and death, and if your plot involves either, don't leave your young reader discouraged.

A good way to find plots that work is to study plot patterns in beloved classics:

Plots for Children Ages Four–Six

Fantasy:
retelling of classic nursery stories (e.g., "The Three Little Pigs")

twisted retelling and fairy tales (e.g., Jane Yolen's original fairy tale *Sleeping Ugly* for "The Sleeping Beauty")

Real life:
journeys to
    the seaside
    grandmother's house
    the woods or mountains
    by boat, plane or train
    the zoo
first night away from home
first day at preschool

Plots for Children Ages Six–Eight

Basic plots:
simple adventure tales
simple quest stories

Plots based on social concerns:
being different from others
making friends if you're timid
adapting to new situations

Fantasy:
science fiction

One of the best ways to plot a story for older children is to play "what if?" with your character:
- What if a boy wants to be an athlete and has an accident?
- What if he has no talent?
- What if he wants to play with dolls?
- What if a girl wants to be a scientist but that career is "not for girls"?
- What if she wants to be ballerina but her parents disapprove?

When your story idea begins to plot itself, develop or change your outline as necessary.

Although your plot outline from beginning through middle to

the end can be thought of as the straight line from cause to effect, your job is to offer information and withhold it in such a way that you create suspense, curiosity, intrigue, all of those things that will keep your reader turning pages. You have to manipulate your plot to achieve these things. But, we repeat, do not manipulate your character!

Reflections on Beginnings

Who should tell your story? Is it to be a first-person narrative or third? What does the reader absolutely have to know in the beginning? Tell only essential facts, the rest can wait. Don't load your beginning with so much information that the plot action is delayed. Place a "hook" in the beginning or middle: a device that will make your surprise ending credible. Here are some ideas for hooks:

character's supernatural or magical power

longing to meet a particular someone (e.g., Santa Claus, love interest)

yearning for a particular thing

need for love/approval

character trait (e.g., shyness, brazenness)

self-image concerns

Middles

They are the most difficult but the most fun. Plot should be building up suspense with obstacles, but it is too easy to let it bog down. The best time to speed the middle onward and upward is when your first draft is done. Draw your plot line and erase any part of the line that is on a plane or going down. Translated into action, that means trim, cut, eliminate everything that doesn't contribute to the cause and effect of your plot. Here are some things to look out for an eliminate as you work:

subplots that go nowhere

unexplained or unnecessary characters

scenes between adult characters not involving the young people

lengthy explanation of how something happened

long-winded scene-setting

author's or narrator's observations or judgment about the action
flashbacks
preaching

Endings

Ask yourself if the ending is satisfying. Is it too predictable? Appropriate to your reader's age? If not true to your original plot outline, is it better? If true to your original plot outline, can you make it better without compromising the integrity of your characters or the setting?

Before you send your book off to a publisher, ask yourself whether your characters are fully developed. Is your setting authentic and interesting? Does the action in your plot develop excitingly and convincingly from character, setting and obstacles to solution? If it needs fixing, fix it.

The following successful books have plots worth analyzing:

Goodnight Moon by Margaret Wise Brown, illustrated by Clement Hurd—A child says good night to the objects in his room.

Millions of Cats by Wanda Gag—A man goes in search of a kitten for his wife and finds among millions of cats the perfect pet.

Curious George by H.A. Rey—A monkey has funny adventures in the city.

If You Give a Mouse a Cookie by Laura Numeroff, illustrated by Felicia Bond—The ultimate cause-and-effect plot.

Madeline by Ludwig Bemelmans—In a French orphanage, a little girl finds love and friendship.

Where the Wild Things Are by Maurice Sendak—A naughty boy sent to his room comes to terms with himself by conquering his emotions masquerading as monsters.

The Napping House by Don and Audrey Wood—A cumulative tale, beautifully illustrated, in which the plot is told pictorially.

The Runaway Bunny by Margaret Wise Brown, illustrated by Clement Hurd—A perfect example of a perfect picture book with barely any plot.

Stone Soup by Marcia Brown—A great retelling of a folktale.

The Story of Ferdinand by Munro Leaf, illustrated by Robert Lawson—A young bull's adventures in Spain develop because he prefers flowers to fighting.

The Tale of Peter Rabbit by Beatrix Potter—A naughty bunny disobeys his mother and barely escapes a farmer's wrath.

Doctor DeSoto by William Steig—One of the great cause-and-effect plots coupled with irresistible, storytelling illustrations.

Mike Mulligan and His Steam Shovel by Virginia Lee Burton—The comeback story of a pair who persevere.

If you are writing for older readers, study the plots of these outstanding books.

Holes by Louis Sachar—Newbery Medal 1998. A troublemaker is sent to summer camp.

Send Me Down a Miracle by Han Nolan—A young country girl who plans to follow her father's footsteps finds she must defy him when an unconventional stranger comes to town.

Shiloh by Phyllis Reynolds Naylor—A young boy is loyal to his dog even in the face of threats from a cruel, drunken neighbor.

Sounder by William H. Armstrong—When his sharecropper father is jailed for stealing food, a young black boy grows in courage and understanding by learning to read and with the help of his devoted dog, Sounder.

The Indian in the Cupboard by Lynne Reid Banks—A nine-year-old boy receives a plastic Indian, a cupboard and a little key for his birthday and finds himself involved in adventure when the Indian comes to life.

A Gathering of Days by Joan W. Blos—Newbery Medal 1980. The journal of a fourteen-year-old girl, kept during the last years she lived on the family farm.

James and the Giant Peach by Roald Dahl—Wonderful adventures abound after James escapes from his fearful aunts by rolling away inside a giant peach.

The Slave Dancer by Paula Fox—Kidnapped by the crew of an Africa-bound ship, a thirteen-year-old boy discovers to his horror that he is on a slaveship.

North to Freedom by Anne Holm—Having escaped from an Eastern European concentration camp where he has spent his life, a twelve-year-old boy struggles to cope with an entirely strange world as he flees northward to freedom in Denmark.

The Lottery Rose by Irene Hunt—A young victim of child abuse gradually overcomes his fears and suspicions when placed in a home with other boys.

The Phantom Tollbooth by Norton Juster—A journey through the land where Milo learns the importance of words and numbers provides a cure for his boredom.

To Kill a Mockingbird by Harper Lee—Eight-year-old Scout Finch tells of life in a small Alabama town where her father, a lawyer, defends a black man charged with raping a white girl.

Good Night, Mr. Tom by Michelle Magorian—A battered child learns to embrace life when he is adopted by an old man in the English countryside during the Second World War.

Hatchet by Gary Paulsen—Newbery Honor Book 1988. After a plane crash, thirteen-year-old Brian spends fifty-four days in the wilderness.

The Light in the Forest by Conrad Richter—After being raised as an Indian for eleven years following his capture at the age of four, John Butler is forcibly returned to his white parents but continues to long for the freedom of Indian life.

Words by Heart by Ouida Sebestyen—A young black girl struggles to fulfill her papa's dream of a better future for their family in the Southwestern town where, in 1910, they are the only blacks.

The Cay by Theodore Taylor—When the freighter on which they are traveling is torpedoed by a German submarine during World War II, an adolescent white boy, blinded by a blow on the head, and an old black man are stranded on a tiny Caribbean island where the boy acquires a new kind of vision, courage and love from his old companion.

Tuck Everlasting by Natalie Babbitt—The Tuck family discovers that a ten-year-old girl and a malicious stranger now share their secret about a spring whose water prevents one from ever growing old.

The Secret Garden by Frances Hodgson Burnett—A boy who has lived as a spoiled invalid regains his health when he and his orphaned cousin restore a once-lovely garden.

The Chocolate War by Robert Cormier—A high-school freshman discovers the devastating consequences of arousing the wrath of the school bullies.

Lord of the Flies by William Golding—Stranded on an island after a plane crash, a group of young boys revert to savagery as they struggle to survive.

Julie of the Wolves by Jean Craighead George—While running away from home and an unwanted marriage, a thirteen-year-old Eskimo girl becomes lost on the North Slope of Alaska and is befriended by a wolf pack.

From the Mixed-Up Files of Mrs. Basil E. Frankweiler by E.L. Konigsburg—Newbery Medal 1968. Two suburban children run away from their Connecticut home and go to New York's Metropolitan Museum of Art, where their ingenuity enables them to live in luxury.

Island of the Blue Dolphins by Scott O'Dell—Newbery Medal 1961. An Indian girl lives alone for eighteen years on an isolated island off the California coast when her tribe emigrated and she was left behind.

The Yearling by Marjorie Kinnan Rawlings—A young boy living in the Florida backwoods is forced to decide the fate of a fawn he has lovingly raised as a pet.

Call It Courage by Armstrong Sperry—Newbery Medal 1941. Based on a Polynesian legend, this is the story of a youth who, though afraid of the sea, sets out alone in his canoe to conquer his fear and prove his courage to himself and his tribe.

The Hundred Dresses by Eleanor Estes—Newbery Honor 1945. In winning a medal she is no longer there to receive, a tight-lipped little Polish girl teaches her classmates a lesson.

Sarah, Plain and Tall by Patricia MacLachlan—Newbery Medal 1968. When their father invites a mail-order bride to come live with them in their prairie home, Caleb and Anna are captivated by their new mother and hope that she will stay.

The Moves Make the Man by Bruce Brooks—A black boy and an emotionally troubled white boy in North Carolina form a precarious friendship.

Ramona the Pest by Beverly Cleary—Ramona is a little sister who always wants to tag along after Beezus and the older kids.

Thursday's Children by Rumer Godden—As he tags along to his spoiled sister's ballet classes, Doone discovers and develops his own rare and special talents.

The Ghost Belongs to Me by Richard Peck—In 1913 in the Midwest, a quartet of characters share adventures from exploding steamboats to exorcising a ghost.

Lost Magic by Berthe Amoss—In the Middle Ages, orphaned Ceridwen learns the art of herbal healing and gains the protection of the local lord until she is accused of witchcraft.

These books with unusual, successful plots are taken from Marigny Dupuy's list of ''Favorite Picture Books'' and Matt Berman's list of ''Favorite Chapter Books and Young Adult Novels.'' Both complete lists appear in *Writing and Illustrating Children's Books for Publication* by Berthe Amoss and Eric Suben. Both Dupuy and Berman are children's book editors for the *Times-Picayune* and both are teachers in elementary schools in New Orleans.

Finally, some basic plot ideas may work equally well for different age groups, through of course they will be developed differently based on the audience. Read the grouped books on the following list and see how you could make your plot work in different formats for readers in different age groups.

Beauty and the Beast by Marianna Mayer
Beauty by Robin McKinley

The Biggest Bear by Lynd Ward
The Yearling by Marjorie Kinnan Rawlings

Noah's Ark by Peter Spier
Many Waters by Madeleine L'Engle

The Tale of Peter Rabbit by Beatrix Potter
Rabbit Hill by Robert Lawson
Watership Down by Richard Adams

Reading these books will show you that plot is more than what happens. It's a complex of character, emotion, setting and theme, each of which can change the color and significance of the bare event. Working out your plot with these elements in mind will help you bring it alive for young readers.

Chapter Seven

Writing

Ideas, characters, plots—these are some of the basic building blocks of your book. But you must also think about the cement that holds them together—the words. Picture books for children are made up of two components—the text and the pictures. Books for older readers may have pictures that are only incidental or even no pictures at all. But no matter what age group you hope to reach with your work, the words are important. You can have a wonderful idea, fascinating characters, an inventive format, a novel setting—but without strong, age-appropriate writing, you will not reach your intended audience.

TITLES

You may feel that the first choice you must make as a writer is your title. In fact, the title is often the last thing about a book to be finalized. The title is a subtle tool—it identifies your book and, one hopes, communicates something important about the story. The title should also, if possible, communicate something about the theme, the idea that motivates the action in your story. And, perhaps most importantly, your title is a marketing tool. It should grab the reader, and it can best do so through the use of one or two words with proven appeal. Finally, a title for a children's book should be short, no more than five words for preference.

Think about the titles of some successful books. *Where the Wild Things Are* is a great picture-book title though on the surface it doesn't seem to tell much. The phrase "wild things" is catchy and resonates with naughty children whose parents have called them wild things. The grammatical structure of the title suggests a question ("where *are* the wild things?") and suggests something mysterious and intriguing.

For young adults, Robert Cormier's *The Chocolate War* is an equally great title. Again, the words themselves don't tell much on the literal level. But the juxtaposition of two intriguing concepts certainly grabs readers.

You may not know what to call your story until you finish it and really understand what it's about. But the title should contain at least one alluring concept that plays an important part. Here are some words that work well in titles of children's books:

Bunny	Magic
Grandpa	First
I	Little
Lucky	Busy
Mystery	Friends
Animals	Sleep
Big	Secret
Best	Runaway
My	Play
Favorite	Nice
Story	Party

Some concepts are so commercial and appealing that they *must* be part of your title if they fit with the concept of your story:

Dinosaur	Numbers
Christmas	ABC
Space	Colors
Bugs	Shapes
Good Night	Sounds
Cars	Dictionary
Trucks	

Although these words are musts, try to be lively and interesting in your title. You could call your book *A Visit to the Dentist*, if that's your topic. But it's much more interesting to do as Jan Wahl did and call it *Timothy Tiger's Terrible Toothache*. You can use these different poetic devices to make your title more appealing:

alliteration (same initial sound)

assonance (similar internal sounds)
dissonance (different internal sounds)
onomatopoeia (words that sound like the thing they describe)
rhyme (internal or terminal)
opposition (juxtaposition of dissimilar ideas)

Another way to make your title—and all your writing—more interesting is to choose nouns that are personal, that communicate what a young character feels rather than merely describing a person or thing. In the following list, note that the subjective words convey the experience from the point of view of the child character. It is by choosing such words that you help yourself see the story from your main character's point of view and help the reader feel the character's feelings.

Objective	Subjective
dentist	toothache
barber	haircut
doctor	sick
classroom	school day
present	surprise

You may hear that your publisher will offer a lot of input about your title, and it is true. But having an appealing title may help you get a publisher to read your manuscript in the first place. Don't be afraid to make the title as obvious as you can. Really emphasize the most commercial aspect of your story in what is, after all, the first bit of your writing most readers will see.

Some publishers say that putting a proper name in the title may limit the book's appeal. However, if you have written a story with anthropomorphic characters, put the animal name in the title. It's sure to add to the book's appeal, especially if you've chosen a cuddly and popular animal:

Bear	Rabbit
Pig	Cow
Cat	Elephant
Puppy	Mouse

NARRATOR

As your title may be subject to lots of discussion and change, the first important choice you really have to make in the writing is deciding who is telling your story. There are three types of narration: first person, second person and third person. A first-person narrator tells the story from his or her own point of view, using the word "I" as the subject of the book. Richard Scarry's *I Am a Bunny* is an example of a picture book for very young children that is told from the point of view of the narrator. Generally, an "I" narrator works best in older fiction, where children can relate to someone self-aware and with a developed sense of consciousness and perspective. The "I" is generally least effective with an animal narrator, as it is difficult to evoke an animal's point of view convincingly.

First-person narration is potentially a very rewarding form for your story. However, you need a well-developed character for the narrator. Excellent examples are Charlotte Brontë's *Jane Eyre* and Mark Twain's *Huckleberry Finn*. Each tells her or his own story. Each author captures the character's voice with amazing virtuosity—you feel that you know the character inside out. Writing this way is a bit like writing an entire book in dialogue—it's a terrific feat of imagination and disciplined writing. In each event that happens, you must be aware of and express the narrator's point of view about:

what happens
the other characters
his own feelings
his own actions
his surroundings
physical setting
language he would really use
interaction with peer group
dealings with authority figures
school environment

Both Jane Eyre and Huckleberry Finn are outcasts in different ways, and that circumstance gives each one an interesting point of view. On the other hand, *Little Women* is told from the point of view

of the third-person narrator. Although Jo is clearly the book's hero-ine and most distinctive character, the novel tells the story of all four sisters and would have an entirely different impact if narrated by the emotional and headstrong, though admittedly loving, Jo. Think whether a first-person narrator really works for the story you are writing. Consider some of the following issues in making this choice:
strong personality
vocabulary choices
need for dialect
sufficient maturity to narrate own story
historical period
male/female protagonist
importance of what happens inside the character
character's reliability as an observer

A different type of first-person narrator appears in E. Nesbit's *The Story of the Treasure Seekers.* The book deals with a family of children left to their own devices after their mother dies and their father becomes preoccupied with money. Oswald is one of the children who narrates the book but the story is told in the third person. This device allows Oswald to praise Oswald throughout—only to reveal his own identity inadvertently in the end! The trick is clever and funny and very revealing of character. Think about what you are trying to convey with your story and how your narrator can help you achieve that goal.

You can tell the reader a tremendous amount of information about your main character by capturing that character's voice and telling the story from her point of view. As you try to imagine the story from the point of view of your first-person narrator, think care-fully about the following aspects:
language he would use (including slang)
what he would know/not know about the story
feelings about other characters
emotions about his own situation
narrator's growth/development as a character
lifestyle
physical location
family situation

aspirations
age relative to other characters
social position
interest in the story's outcome

Because of the wide variety of settings and characters available to the author of a children's book, the first-person narrator can present a truly unusual perspective. If thoroughly imagined and well executed, such narration can be entertaining and fun for both author and reader. Think about your story as told from the perspective of:

space alien	naughty child
animal character	younger/older sibling
pet	school bully
fairy	school misfit
monster	class clown
infant	doll or other toy
teacher	

The second person is, in a sense, the reader narrating. Here is an example of a children's books narrated in second person:

> You woke up this morning. And what did you do? You got out of bed!
> You ran downstairs to the kitchen. And what did mama give you? Cereal!

The "you" is somewhat limiting and will be unconvincing for the many children whose experience does not very closely resemble the experience of the child in the book. The second-person narrator is extremely unusual and probably limited to use in books for very small children. However, a well-known example of second-person writing is the old McGuffey Readers, with sentences like:

> See Spot run! Run, Spot, run!

The implied subject of the first sentence is a "you."
By far the most widespread narrator in children's books, as in

most books is the omniscient, third-person narrator. This is the narrator who sees all and tells all. From Beatrix Potter's *The Tale of Peter Rabbit* to Maurice Sendak's *Where the Wild Things Are*, the third-person narrator is everywhere. He calls people by their names and tells the reader where they went, how they looked and what they did. But this narrator must be a convincing character, too, even if he is invisible. He must stay focused on the main action of the story and convey the shifts of emotion through modulations of voice.

Sometimes the omniscient narrator may be a character in the story, one whose role is incidental but allows her to observe all the action and have a good understanding of the main characters' feelings and thought processes. Ellen in Emily Bronte's *Wuthering Heights* is this type of narrator. Even if your narrator never makes it into the action of the story, though, it may help you write if you cast yourself in the role of the narrator. Thus, the narrator could be:

A Sympathetic Adult

parent	teacher
grandparent	clergy member
other relative	housekeeper
neighbor	baby-sitter

Another Child

sibling	neighbor
friend	playmate
classmate	

CHARACTER NAMES

Although your omniscient narrator may not have a name, your characters will. Thinking of names for your characters will help make them real to you and real to your readers, especially if you use names children will recognize from real life. Here are some variants for the important characters likely to be found between the covers of a children's book:

Mother

mama	mami
ma	moms
mommy	

Father

tdada	papi
da	pop
pa	daddy
papa	

Grandfather

grandpa	pops
gramps	abuelo
grampy	paga

Grandmother

granny	gran
grandma	maga
abuela	nana
grammy	

If you're writing a contemporary book, the names of your child characters should be modern. Here are some that today's child might recognize:

Boys

Jake	Leo
Jason	Josh
Troy	Henry
Tyler	Jackson
Dylan	Thor
Zack	Max
Andreas	Coltrane

Alyosha	Eli
Muhammed	

Girls

Taryn	Jenny
Whitney	Emma
Leora	Carly
Corey	Nita
Brittany	Zoe
Courtney	Keyana
Heather	Juliet
Kylie	Clara
Sophie	

When writing about nonparental adult characters, such as teachers, nannies and other caregivers, remember that nowadays children are likely to call such individuals by their first names.

PRONOUNS

One of the many paradoxes of children's books is that the writing is designed to be processed by more than one audience at a time. Picture books are generally read aloud by parents to young children. The text therefore must "read" well, as a poem or play should. And when read aloud, the text should be crystal clear, without unclear antecedents for pronouns, complicated sentence structures and sophisticated vocabulary that stops the flow both of articulating and of understanding. An antecedent, of course, is the specific noun that you refer to when you use a pronoun later in the sentence. In the following sentence, the antecedent is "flower," and the pronoun is "it":

The flower is red and it grows in the yard.

The most common pronouns used as subjects of sentences or phrases are the following:

it	they
he	we
she	

The most common pronouns used as adjectives generally describe possession of a thing by a person whose identity must be clear from the context:

his	my
her	your
their	whose
our	

A big problem with pronouns is unclear antecedents. For instance, read this sentence:

She cut the bread and the cheese and ate it.

Does "it" refer to the bread, or to the cheese, or to the combination? You cannot really tell, and that means there is an unclear antecedent. Another thing to keep in mind is that the antecedent should always come before the pronoun. For instance:

Because he did not like it, he threw away the sandwich.

The previous sentence is less clear than the obvious alternative:

Because he did not like the sandwich, he threw it away.

In the first sentence, the meaning of "it" is unclear. In the second sentence, you can't mistake that the sandwich is "it."

Finally, another word about "it." Flabby writing is often marked by the use of "it" as the subject of a sentence. Here is an example:

It was a beautiful day.

The obvious question is, *What* was a beautiful day? The pronoun has no antecedent, nor can it have a logical one, because a beautiful day is a beautiful day and nothing else. In good writing, every word counts. Eliminate every "it" where a clearer, more elegant solution can be found. The sentence could be rewritten thus:

The day was beautiful.

The sentence could also become a clause that introduces a sentence and eliminates the need for "it":

On a beautiful day, Johnny roller-skated to town.

As with all rules, there are exceptions to the rule against using "it" as the subject of a sentence. A completely indefinite "it" can be:

raining	morning
snowing	bedtime
sunny	hot
windy	cold
dark	cloudy
light	lunchtime
nighttime	

If you wish to express a general state of being, "it" may be the only appropriate subject for your sentence, even without an antecedent. But try writing your story without that little word, and you may find you become much more inventive. "Bright drops fell from the sky" beats "It was raining"—wouldn't you agree?

SENTENCE STRUCTURE

Here is another general rule crucial to good writing for children and young people: One thought per sentence. For the most part, it is best to avoid compound or other complex sentences. Part of your job is helping children glean meaning from words. You can help with this goal by keeping your writing simple and uncluttered. If the sentence needs a comma anywhere but before or after attributions of dialogue, think about breaking it up into two sentences. Of course, variety can be a hallmark of good prose style, and compound sentences or subordinate clauses may occasionally be desirable or even necessary. But as a general rule, try to keep it simple. Here are good single thoughts for single sentences:

introducing protagonist by name and one trait

describing an action
setting the scene
what a character said
how the protagonist felt
where a character went
why an action was performed

This thought leads to another topic of great importance for all writers—the use of clichés. Clichés are tried-and-true usages that people employ all the time in conversation and in writing. Clichés often start life as clear, creative images to describe common phenomena. The phrase is so apt and universally recognizable that people begin to use it all the time. Here are a few clichés:

sly as a fox	sweet as candy
fast as a rabbit	dull as paint
fat as a pig	shiny as a new penny
faithful as a dog	red as a beet
through the roof	in hot water
brave as a lion	hot as blazes
high as a kite	screaming like a banshee
timid as a mouse	light as air
gentle as a lamb	fresh as a daisy
bright as day	good as gold
cute as a bug	at a snail's pace

Basically, these are stock phrases that come to the writer's mind—and pen—whenever he wants to vivify a simple description. When writing for children, clichés are best avoided. First, the phrases may be new to much of your young audience, so familiarity will not be an aid to understanding. Second, small children do not have a wide range of associations to use in understanding the image. Finally, your own interesting and vivid description may be much more appealing and appropriate. Instead of "Joe's face turned as red as a beet," why not try "Joe's face turned as red a bowl full of cherry Jell-O"? For better or worse, children are probably more familiar with Jell-O than with beets anyway.

Nevertheless, there are some clichés that are irreplaceable and would be missed, even by the smallest children, if they were absent. These stock phrases grow out of the oral tradition of storytelling and signal important things to the reader, such as when the story is beginning and when it is ending. The Greek poet Homer sang his epics aloud, so his standard phrases about rosy-fingered Dawn painting the sky, and the wine-dark sea, were important signals to his listeners. Similarly, "once upon a time" and "they lived happily ever after" are important moments for the hearer of a fairy tale and should always be included. In your modern, original children's story, ending with the words "good night" may be equally important and effective.

Careful reading of the picture books of Margaret Wise Brown can teach you a lot about inventive, *un*-cliché descriptions. Here is a mix-and-match list of nouns and adjectives from her writing. Try different combinations and see which ones sound both fun and meaningful:

Adjective	Noun
green	bugs
shiny	wood
warm	ferns
wild	geranium
pink	song
wind-blown	ears
old	baby
tangled	ground
brown	bog
gray	mushrooms
frail	river
warm	dandelions
sweet	shadow
bouncy	air

Writing a picture book is very much like writing a poem, as some of the combinations in this list demonstrate. However, any comparison you make must have meaning, and the meaning must be comprehensible by a child. Children have limited vocabularies and so often use unexpected words for things. You can do the same provided you do so with a child's logic.

Here is an outtake from a book of original poems for children:

> Night's coming soon.
> I wait for the moon,
> Which descends from the sky like a giant cocoon.

The editor's marginal comment was: "How does a giant cocoon descend? And whence?" This remark was a highfalutin way of communicating to the writer that the comparison was essentially meaningless. Don't ever write nonsense, even when you are writing nonsense. Study the extraordinary logic of Lewis Carroll's *Alice in Wonderland* or the outstanding versification of Edward Lear's nonsense poems for models of excellent craftsmanship in the service of whimsy. Consider some of these options as you write your whimsical story:

animal characters behaving like humans
animal characters' pets
animal characters' interaction with humans
speech
magical substances/powers
unusual creatures
where things come from
transformation of everyday objects

Writing in children's books must be concrete. That means you are somewhat limited in your choices, as many metaphors are likely to be lost on your literal young readers. But the limitation may be very freeing and help you improve your writing by forcing you to focus on information you can perceive with your five senses. When writing, focus on describing things as they appear and not by comparing them with other things. Here are some examples of specific, easily pictured noun phrases.

a tiny girl	the big green leaf
the sweetest voice	a big blanket
an ugly toad	the pleasant sunshine
the muddy bank	a blue lake
a wide brook	

In addition to lucid word choice, lucid sentence structure is very important. A complete sentence must have at least a noun and a verb. Make sure the subject and verb agree. This means that a singular noun gets a singular verb. Confusion occurs when the subject of a sentence is a group. A group is singular although it is made up of plural individuals. Thus:

	Correct Verb	
A number of books	is	on the table.
Several books	are	on the table.
A group of ducks	is	crossing the street.
Some ducks	are	crossing the street.
The happy family	lives	in the house.
The family members	live	in the house.

British usage is sometimes different from American and may require sentences like "The happy family live in the house." However, if you are writing for an American audience, use an American-style guide (e.g., Strunk and White's *The Elements of Style*).

It is important that you write in complete sentences. The following sentence is complete:

Spunky ran.

However, most sentences convey more information than that. The sentence tells *who* and *what*. You could complete the sentence by asking yourself some of the important questions asked by news reporters:

how   when

why   where

Here are some of the sentences you could make by answering these questions.

Spunky ran as fast as he could.
Spunky ran because the big dog was after him.

Spunky ran through the night.
Spunky ran down the street.

These are good, clear, simple sentences that would fit well in a book for children.

It is a rule of thumb in children's books that one sentence should convey one thought. Compound sentences are generally to be avoided. Compound sentences are those comprising two independent clauses joined by "and" or "but." However, variety is important, and meaning and context must rule the day. Here are some complex sentences broken down into child-friendly complete correct sentences. The most satisfying sentences to write and to read are complete thoughts, grammatically expressed, yet simple and direct.

Spunky ran and ran until he came to a big stream, which he swam across as fast as he could.
Spunky ran and ran. Soon he came to a big stream. He swam across as fast as he could.

Sally couldn't wait to get to school because she knew she would meet her friend Joan, and today was Joan's birthday.
Sally couldn't wait to get to school. She knew she would meet her friend Joan. And today was Joan's birthday!

Belinda the witch straddled her broomstick and soared off into the sky, searching for toads, toadstools and newts.
Belinda the witch straddled her broomstick. She soared off into the sky. She was looking for toads, toadstools and newts.

Although one misses some of the headlong rush of the compound versions, the second versions are generally much clearer, especially if one is hearing them read aloud. Note that in breaking up the sentences, you create the need for transitional words. These words are perfectly correct at the beginning of sentences and are educational in helping instruct your young reader in time sequencing, logic and cause and effect. Here are some of these transitional words:

and	also
but	later
so	soon
for	before long
then	after a while
but	

DIALOGUE

But just breaking long sentences up is not enough to make interesting writing. As your picture book will be read aloud, the writing of it presents an unbeatable opportunity to provide captivating dialogue. The adult reader may relish the chance to try out different voices in play-acting the book to his child audience. The child listener will certainly be charmed by characterful dialogue. And you can express so much more about the characters through their own words than you can through dry narration.

> "Look at that little dog go!" shouted Mr. Smithers. Spunky swam across the stream and kept on running.

> "I wish the schoolbus would come," Sally thought. She couldn't wait to see Joan.
> Today was Joan's birthday!

> "Hee-hee-hee!" Belinda cackled as she straddled her broomstick. Soaring into the sky, she sang, "Toads, toadstools, and newts—perfect for my witch's brew!"

Look for opportunities to write dialogue when you find yourself with one of the following situations:
- describing what a character thinks
- telling what a character said instead of giving the quote
- introducing a personality trait
- showing a relationship
- expressing a feeling

- responding to an important piece of information
- feeling a sensation
- reacting to others

Of course, dialogue means being aware of the words a character would actually use. In coming up with those words, you must keep in mind some of the following factors about your character:

age	historical period
education	social class
ethnic background	personality traits
situation	emotions
sex	

When you write dialogue, you must be aware of the verbs you use to attribute speeches to the different characters. Many writers make the mistake of trying to vary a chain of "he said"s and "she said"s by introducing other verbs of attribution. However, many of these verb choices are incorrect and even silly. For instance, "he laughed." People often write sentences like the following:

"I can't wait to go," he laughed.

Well, just you try laughing and speaking clearly at the same time. It cannot be done. A better variant, though more wordy, is:

"I can't wait to go," he said with a laugh.

The following are further verbs of attribution that should be avoided:

coughed	giggled
sang	snickered
trilled	growled
sneezed	groaned
sighed	moaned

Here are a few exotic verbs of attribution that may work in the right context:

blurted	shrieked
sputtered	whined
grumped	complained
grouched	joked
griped	hissed (if the sentence in-
whispered	cludes several sibilants)
spoke up	bellowed
mumbled	sputtered
shouted	told
screamed	chattered
muttered	

Nevertheless, there is no substitute for the simple word *said*, which always says what it means. It can always be complemented with an adverb or an adverbial phrase to make it more expressive of the way in which the speech was said.

When writing about animal characters, you may be tempted to use clever, animal-appropriate words to convey that they are speaking. Don't. If you are creating a convincing fantasy world in which sheep and cows can talk, don't mess it up with strange verbs like:

mooed	meowed
baaed	roared
chirped	purred
howled	twittered
barked	

Avoid redundancies. A common usage, but one to be avoided, is "he thought to himself." The phrase is redundant and also silly. Thinking is an action complete in itself, and it is not done "to" anyone or anything else, including oneself. Look for other places to edit and refine your writing where you repeat something already implicit in your text.

DICTION

As with verbs of attribution, so with all your word choices. They should be simple and concrete, not lavish and peculiar. The following list gives simple, concrete words that may be more meaningful to children than their more difficult synonyms:

Nouns

door	portal
car	automobile
woods	forest
baby	infant
picture	photograph
trip	journey
pan	skillet
tool	utensil
truck	vehicle

Verbs

speed	accelerate
want	desire
love	adore
win	succeed
read	recite
talk	orate
fry	sauté

Adjectives

huge	gigantic
great	terrific
tasty	delicious
happy	delirious
chatty	talkative
clear	crystalline
hard	difficult

Of course, word choice, or diction, must be determined by situation and speaker. If the character speaking is a parent or teacher, it might be unconvincing for the dialogue to include only simple words. In such a situation, the context demands that more sophisticated vocabulary be used. At such times, take extra care to make sure the meaning of the big words is clear from the context.

Often generic words work better in picture books than specific words. This is because children may know the general word for something but not the specific. Moreover, using a generic may give the illustrator more license to create a wonderful scene. Remember that the picture book text is not final until the paintings are done. If it makes more sense to use "rose" instead of flower after the illustrator has his way, the word can be changed. But saying "rose" at the outset, unless necessary to the meaning of the story, may limit the illustrator's choices. Here are good generic nouns to use:

tree	picture
bush	animal
flower	cloud
plant	tooth
dog	gem
cat	fruit
car	vegetable
truck	dish
house	fish
skirt	bird
dress	tool
rock	dance

The exception here is in using specific nouns for things children know a lot about. For instance, food or candy words can be frustrating if too vague. If the context is appropriate, feel free to use these specifics:

chocolate	pudding
vanilla	birthday cake
gumdrop	cotton candy
lollipop	apple
hot dog	pear

popcorn   banana
ice cream   lamb chop

Use good active verbs. The trick in children's books is to use as few words as possible. We always advise writers to avoid adverbs and adjectives where possible. So instead of saying "He ran quickly," say "he sped." Here are some others:

walked fast	jogged
ate greedily	gobbled
spoke quickly	gabbled
eyed greedily	ogled
looked angry	scowled
walked across	crossed
slept lightly	dozed
moved gingerly	tiptoed
crept slowly	crawled
came together	gathered
was restles	swiggled
laughed lightly	giggled
dripped slowly	trickled
grew quiet	hushed

In today's world, be conscious of using gender-neutral words when describing occupations. Also choose the most up-to-date appellations for members of minority groups:

mail carrier	delivery person
police officer	African American
firefighter	Asian American
sanitation worker	Native American
server	Mexican American

While it's good to use general nouns, avoid adjectives and adverbs because they are often too vague. For instance, here is a sentence we used before as an example while discussing pronouns:

The day was beautiful.

Does this sentence say as much as it could, especially to a young child? Ask yourself, what made the day beautiful? Instead of a vague adjective, you can use the following nouns and verbs:

The sun shone.

The sky was blue.

The sky was clear.

The air was warm on Terry's face.

Not a cloud was in the sky.

Sunshine drenched the earth.

The trees rustled in the breeze.

Birds sang in the trees.

The scent of ripe strawberries rose through the air.

The day was made for lemonade and cherry ice.

The use of specifics helps the reader visualize the scene and helps you write a more interesting story. To make your writing more interesting while avoiding the use of dull adjectives and adverbs, try using your five senses to describe what's happening.

- how does it look?
- how does it sound?
- how does it smell?
- how does it feel?
- how does it taste?

Ask yourself these questions every time you find yourself grabbing for a dull old adjective or adverb. Here are some vivid verbs that imply something about how things look, feel, taste, smell or feel.

burned	ruffled
froze	patted
basked	sniffed
shivered	startled
boiled	struck
trembled	whistled
steamed	sang
stiffened	crunched
smoothed	squished

Some adjectives cannot be avoided. For instance, colors can be expressed only one way. However, even with colors you can try to replace the obvious adjective with your own combination of words. For instance, instead of saying "The fog was light gray," how about "mist rose the color of a pearl"? Here are strong adjectives that would be missed from children's books:

good	yellow
bad	green
wicked	wet
royal	dry
happy	open
sad	closed
red	pretty
black	bored
white	awful
blue	

VERSE

Many children's writers aspire to write in verse. There are several things to know about writing in verse. You must strive for true rhymes. A true rhyme is one where the final syllables of the rhyming words truly rhyme. True rhymes are important but difficult to find. A close call is not good enough. Here is a sampling of false rhymes that are close but don't quite make it:

lock/socks
men/friend
soon/boom
October/over
Monday/someday
food/good
wilderness/princess

Here are several true rhymes:
fox/socks
men/ten
send/tend

plant/can't
November/remember
Monday/Sunday
food/sued

Some rhymes occupy the borderline, depending how you say them. Margaret Wise Brown once rhymed these two words: Squirrel/whirl. A New Yorker would have to say "squirrel" in a slightly unusual way to make the rhyme work. A Midwesterner could make the words rhyme with no effort at all.

It is also important that the verse scan. That means you should have approximately the same number of syllables in each line or set of lines. Moreover, the stressed syllables must fall in the same place in each line. Robert Louis Stevenson, in *A Child's Garden of Verses*, wrote the following lines that scan perfectly:

> The world is so full of a number of things,
> I'm sure we should all be as happy as kings.

Each line has eleven syllables, and the same syllables in each line are stressed. (A quick look through the collection will reveal nothing but true rhymes, as well.) Here are two lines of poetry that do not scan:

> Hello, Jenny, hello!
> You are very nice to know.

The first line has six syllables, the second has eight. This defect is not fatal so long as the next set of lines also alternates six and eight syllables with stresses in the same places.

EXCLAMATIONS

As with all rules, there are exceptions to the rules in this chapter. One exception often seen in children's books is the one-word or two-word sentence. Such a sentence is not a sentence in the true sense but is an exclamation that heightens the feelings of the story. Here are several examples from published books:

Yum!	Uh-oh!
Wow!	Splash!
Boom!	Thump!
Hurray!	Zoom!
Hush!	Wheee!
Oh, no!	Christmas Eve!
Oops!	Toys!

USE WORDS THAT SHOW

Here is another fun exception: When you write dialogue, what comes between the quotation marks needn't follow any rules. It can be ungrammatical, spelled oddly to indicate dialect, one word, two words—anything that person would actually say.

The great benefit of dialogue is that it allows you to show a character rather than describing the character at length in a way that would be less efficient and less clear to the reader. In your writing, always strive to show rather than tell. Don't tell the reader that a girl was pretty; say "She had long golden hair." Look at these other examples of ways to show rather than tell.

On a warm spring day, Kate walked to town.
Kate felt the sun on her face as she strolled to town.

Pete stepped up to the plate and swung the bat.
Pete's heart thumped as he took his stance. WHOOSH! He swung.

Ms. Crabb did not like Suzie's dog Spunky.
"Get that dog out of my flower bed," Ms. Crabb snapped as Suzie picked up Spunky.

Grandma was always very kind and loving to the children.
The smell of fresh-baked cookies wafted through the open door of Grandma's kitchen.

Even with the aid of pictures, it is not enough for your words to tell what happened. Each sentence must be imagined with characters and emotions in mind. Dialogue, strong word choices and concrete scene-setting are your tools in crafting words that make your story come alive. And the ingredients of good writing are the same whatever your audience. As readers get older, you can choose sophisticated words more of the time, use complex sentence structures more often than rarely, and paint the settings with your words. But simplicity and ease of understanding should always be your goals. So go ahead and have fun! Keeping in mind the age of your readers and that the best communication is always the clearest, your only limitations are your imagination and the rules of grammar.

Chapter Eight

Thinking Visually

Think of your children's book as a movie. You are the director! You should try to visualize every detail of your book, even if you are not the illustrator. In writing a picture book, you must craft text that gives firm guidance to the illustrator regarding what to show. In your young-adult book, you must paint the entire picture through your words.

Visual details are important in children's books. Although, as discussed in chapter seven, you do not want to limit the choices available to your illustrator, you must provide enough specifics to allow him—and the reader—to visualize the scene as you do. One of the great shortcomings of many children's book manuscripts is that they are not strongly visualized. You must consider a number of things in imagining the illustrations for each page of your book: character, setting, action. But you must also imagine your book in lots of detail. Here are interesting things to include in scenes, as appropriate:

Food

cookies	apple
lollipops	orange
hot cocoa	mashed potatoes
birthday cake	American cheese
oatmeal	baloney sandwich
milk	grape juice

Playthings

helium balloons	Teddy bear
scooter	crayons

building blocks	toy truck
erector set	red wagon
pail and shovel	wooden sled

Things Found at Special Events/Places

fireworks display	topiary trees
feast	ice sculptures
oompah band	punch bowl
singing Christmas tree	streamers
miniature train	swan boats

Special Clothing

nightshirt	hobo costume
mob cap	waders
yarmulke	tutu
choir robe	all-weather gear
Santa suit	kilt

As stated earlier, your words are the glue that hold your book together. However, in a picture book, the pictures are what keep the action moving and the attention focused. You can help your writing tremendously, and also help your illustrator, by including in your manuscript a verbal description of the scene you picture in your mind's eye as you write. In describing the pictures in words, here are things to include:

weather	plants or trees
facial expression	animals
clothing	room
shoes	building/structure
food	furniture
colors	view
number of things	vehicle

POINT OF VIEW

Your first concern in framing the picture is point of view. Like a filmmaker, you must think about the focus of your shot and the cropping. Cropping is cutting around the sides of a picture to focus on the most essential elements. Just as in writing, you need a point of view for the pictures. The point of view can be an omniscient pictorial narrator's perspective or that of a particular character. From whose point of view is the shot being made? If from that of a specific character, look through that character's eyes. What would the character be seeing at this point in the story? Think about scenic elements:

couch	cityscape
bed	landscape
table	painting
desk	picture
dishes	building
pots	car
tableware	truck
window	bus
door	airplane
sky	boat
tree	land
bush	beach
flower	desert
sea	forest
lake	sign
stream	billboard
woods	bicycle
river	tricycle
bridge	fence
animal	

LIGHT AND WEATHER

A cinematographer must think about the light he has for photographing and the weather conditions when filming outdoors. You should think about these things, too. Light and weather can be expressive of emotion and could subtly communicate mood to the reader, as well as foreshadowing developments in the plot. Here are some options.

Light

dark	smoky
bright	moonlight
gloomy	starlight
murky	sunlight
dim	dusk
gray	twilight
wintry	half-light
hazy	

Weather

rain	clear
snow	ice
sleet	dry
hail	moist
fog	hurricane
mist	tornado
drizzle	gale
wind	thunderstorm
bluster	tidal wave
clouds	typhoon

FOCUS

You must choose a focus of interest for the picture. Is the focus a character? Is it a scenic element? What is necessary to show to convey the sense of this part of the story? For instance, at the beginning of the fairy tale of "The Sleeping Beauty," it might be important to have an establishing shot of the castle where the young princess is born. Such niceties can add dimension to your book. In the case of "The Sleeping Beauty," showing the castle at the beginning adds a dramatic contrast later when you show the sleeping castle surrounded by briars. In addition, conceiving of the first page or spread of your retelling in this way will certainly alter what you write on the first page. Here are a few ideas for beginning your book, where you probably want to emphasize the most important feature of your story:

Panoramic View

city	country
town	building
house	zoo
school	circus
world	farm

Cross Section (inside shown)

skyscraper	cottage
bus	castle
haunted house	egg
pyramid	Earth
tree	habitat
human body	

Portrait

family	pet
class	animals in barn
hero	tribe
team	herd of animals
club	school of fish
choir	friends

CHARACTERS

Most scenes will have characters in them. First, visualize your primary characters. What do they look like? Although in most cases the illustrator will have most license in determining the appearance of your characters, your ability to see them in your mind's eye will help make them real for you and reveal some important characteristics that should find their way into the pictures.

Skin

pale	café au lait
freckled	sunburnt

olive
pink
ruddy
brown
tanned

leathery
wrinkled
withered
bronze

Eyes

blue
brown
hazel
gray
green
violet

black
bloodshot
red
big
little
copper

Hair

brown
blond
yellow
red
auburn
chestnut
honey blond
ash blond
silver

gray
salt-and-pepper
bald
beard
mustache
black
strawberry
straw-colored

Body Build

fat
skinny
stocky
slim
slender
thin
tubby
stout

solid
wraithlike
bony
fleshy
muscular
athletic
tall
short

Fingers

stocky	pudgy
sausagelike	dainty
slender	blunt
tapered	

If your characters are anthropomorphic animals, you should try to work within the limitations of their natural anatomies. Consider the characteristics of the animal you want to use and make sure you can work within these constraints and make your character do all the things he needs to do. Remember some of the following facts:

- Some cows have horns.
- Raccoons have fingers.
- Monkeys have prehensile tails.
- Bears can stand on two legs.
- Polar bears swim.
- Penguins swim.
- All spiders do not spin webs.
- Flying squirrels glide.
- Gorillas build nests in trees.
- Some baby spiders eat their mothers.
- Bats navigate by sound.
- Fireflies' flashes are mating signals.
- Some wasps make paper.
- Otters use rocks to open clam shells.
- Pandas are unsociable.

Think about the characters who are particularly important at this point in the story, of course. But think also about others whose presence might tell the reader something, even though those people are not actively involved in the scene. In other words, think ahead to the action that is coming next. If two children are talking but Mommy overhears them and comments in the next frame, it might be useful to have Mommy coming into the frame illustrating the children's conversation. Sometimes the "extra" person is a character in the story. Sometimes such individuals are like the "extras" in your movie.

Like a movie director, be thinking about the entire scene and who would be there in real life. Here are some passersby who may become important:

School

children	crossing guard
teachers	hall monitor
librarian	coach
principal	schoolbus driver
custodian	cafeteria worker

Home

parent	dog
grandparent	housekeeper
caregiver	gardener
brother	sibling
sister	delivery person
cat	mail carrier

Street

adults	bus driver
children	truck driver
police officers	construction worker
storekeepers	vendor
delivery persons	performer
drivers	

CLOTHING

As in any medium where a story is told principally through visual means, you must think about the entire picture, including the costumes worn by your characters. Costumes can convey important facts about characters—a uniform may immediately convey the type of work a person does. Tidy clothes may indicate a careful person, where untidy clothes may indicate someone in need of better organization.

The following costume choices may help you to visualize your characters:

crown	shawl
cape	baseball cap (worn
robe	backward?)
nurse's uniform	in-line skates
tutu	figure skates
coverall	hockey skates
artist's smock	team jersey
beret	overalls
kneesocks	straw hat
kilt	bandanna
tam	pinafore
chef's toque	wig
apron	mask
toe shoes	bunting
riding boots	rain boots
T-shirt	yellow slicker
diaper	rain hat
underpants	baseball mitt
wedding gown	boxing gloves
christening gown	mittens
tallit	backpack
yarmulke	fanny pack

Remember to be modern in your choices. Today, shoes for young children close with Velcro more often than with shoelaces. Children use digital watches and play computer games.

PROPS

Props may also be important. Props are things your characters carry, hold and manipulate in order to further the action of the story. Props may be as reflective of character as costumes. In the world of classical painting, a person holding a drill and block of wood is a carpenter, regardless of dress. The following props may be equally expressive of your characters' lives.

pen	flag
pencil	garland
ruler	fishing pole
paintbrush	letter
crayon	broom
palette	tuba
doll	flashlight
puppet	basket
trowel	chalk
shovel	baseball bat
spade	telescope
snowball	scissors
umbrella	magic wand
parasol	computer mouse
fan	portable CD player
rope	

EXTRAS

In stories with anthropomorphic characters, be consistent with the types of animals found in the setting you have chosen. In other words, domesticated farm animals would not be found in woodland setting. Here are some of the "extras" who can populate your different animal settings:

Farm

horse	goat
cow	pig
chicken	goose
mule	duck
donkey	bull
dog	rooster
cat	mouse
sheep	rat

Woods

frog	bear
toad	raccoon
fox	snake
mole	squirrel
deer	skunk
field mouse	hedgehog
muskrat	chipmunk
opossum	wolf
rabbit	

Underwater

fish	crab
octopus	stingray
shark	tortoise
whale	snail
clam	eel
oyster	sea horse
lobster	

Jungle

lion	gazelle
tiger	monkey
elephant	gorilla
zebra	baboon

Insect World

butterfly	flea
moth	ant
caterpillar	grasshopper
worm	cricket
bee	locust
spider	firefly

Of course, whether your characters are human or animal, they may be performing actions of all kinds. This will be dictated by your story. Picture books work best when there is action on each page that can be shown in an interesting picture. They work least well when the characters are merely engaged in conversation or cogitation. You must show your characters doing something at all times, even when the sense of the story is being conveyed through dialogue or interior monologue. Here are some things your characters can be shown doing while thinking or talking. Preferably, the action will be suited to the dialogue or interior monologue going on at the same time.

bicycling	brushing teeth
gardening	performing
playing ball	farming
getting dressed	flying kite
walking to school	drawing
riding in a car	skating
singing	climbing
dancing	hiding
walking the dog	playing dress-up
cleaning house	masquerading
cooking	racing
fishing	pushing a carriage
making a present	swinging
attending a party	wading
swimming	seesawing
shopping	building in sand
moving house	picnicking
eating pizza	

EXPRESSION/GESTURE

All the while your character is engaged in these interesting activities, she must register some emotional response to her surroundings and actions. This is where your story takes on drama and meaning for the reader. Knowing what the action means to the principal character helps the reader derive meaning from the story. As an actor expresses emotion through expression and gesture, so must your picture-book character.

Facial Expression

smile	close eyes
frown	widen eyes
grimace	gape
grin	smirk
wink	pucker
blink	blush
cry	blanch
weep	scowl
wrinkle nose	sneer
turn up nose	glower

Gesture/Body Language

shrug	scratch head
hug	pose
kiss	preen
hands on hips	tiptoe
arms crossed	stomp
legs crossed	display
sprawl	kick
straddle	hit
stride	tear
wriggle	smack
shiver	pinch
point	turn back
roll eyes	clench fist
finger to lips	

HOLIDAY THEMES

Now think about the specifics of your story, especially where and when it takes place. In any special time or place, there will be special items you will want to show in the background. Even the characters' clothes may vary by the time of day, time of year and physical setting. In today's crowded children's book market, for instance, holiday themes are popular because holiday seasons are times when adults buy gifts for children. Think about some of these choices as you write your holiday-themed book.

Valentine's Day

scissors	crayons
construction paper	heart-shaped candies
lace doilies	red clothing
chocolate	mailbox
envelopes	cupcakes

Easter

eggs	chocolate eggs/bunnies
baskets	jellybeans
green excelsior	crocuses
dye	bonnets
vinegar	prayer books
bunnies	stained glass
marshmallow chicks	

Passover

seder plate	cooked egg
haggadah	green vegetable
candles	charoseth
Cup of Elijah	yarmulke
Cup of Miriam	cushion
lamb shank bone	

Fourth of July

sky rockets	parchment documents
bottle rockets	picnic blanket
Roman candles	hot dogs
sparklers	lemonade
red-white-and-blue cake	swimming trunks
flags	shorts
powdered wigs	sandals

Halloween

pumpkins
jack-o'-lanterns
autumn leaves
treat bags
sheets
masks
candy corn
candy apples
apple cider

donuts
popcorn
bonfires
makeup
chalk
toilet paper
shaving cream
apples

Thanksgiving

Pilgrim hats
buckle shoes
cranberries
harvest wreath
Indian corn
cotton beards

hasty pudding
chrysanthemums
football
fireplace
turkey

Hanukkah

menorah
candles
dreidel
latkes

applesauce
chocolate coins
cookies
jelly donuts

Christmas

Santa wall-hanging
birthday cake for Jesus
angel decoration for
    treetop
evergreens on table
electric trains
hot chocolate
bells

sleigh
candle centerpiece
tree skirt
tree stand
chestnuts
gingerbread men
grab bag

Kwanzaa

Seven Principles
    Unity
    Self-determination
    Collective work and responsibility
    Cooperative economics
    Purpose
    Creativity
    Faith
straw mat (mkeka)
candleholder (kinara)
seven candles (mshumaa)
ear of corn (muhindi)
red, black and green flag
Unity Cup

Thinking visually as you write is one of the most important things you can do to make your children's book come alive. The book, like a play or movie, is truly a visual medium, and the writer is the individual with the vision of the whole. Let there be no limits on your imagination as you cast, light, costume and dress each scene. Your story will become as colorful and dramatic as you want it to be.

VERY YOUNG READERS

In easy-to-read books, the pictures are still important and must be clear and provide visual clues to allow young readers to gauge their own progress. Humor is often an important ingredient in pictures in easy-to-read books. Here are some sources of visual humor that may be worth building into your story:
    contrasting shapes and sizes
    fat/scrawny
    tall/short
    weird hair
    outlandish clothes
    clothes on animal

gross-out food
landing on rump
getting wet/dirty/muddy
kiss
strange monsters
exaggerated facial expressions
mess
babies/younger siblings
pratfalls (e.g., tripping on banana peel)

OLDER READERS

You must think visually even if you are writing books for older readers.
What pictures are to picture books, verbal descriptions are to middle-grade and young-adult books. Instead of writing out notes for the
illustrator, as you may in a picture book, the word pictures become
part of your story. Here are some categories of things that older
readers love to "see" as they read:

Food

browned meat	fluffy mashed potatoes
steaming vegetables	black bread
golden-brown pancakes	crusty toasted marshmallows

Hair

shiny	straight
sleek	slicked-back
punk	poofy
curly	bun
unruly	

Home Furnishings

velvet draperies	fireplace
wing chair	soup pot
breakfront	hat stand
bric-a-brac	wooden tub

Clothing

blue sash	pink bows
violet silk	yellow bonnet
carved fan	rose velvet ribbon
green umbrella	

Landscape

green grass fields	prairie violets
Indian paintbrush	wild rose buds
blue-eyed grass	rock cliffs
blue flax	huge black cloud

When writing for the young-adult readers, "thinking visually" can be your shorthand phrase for thinking with all your senses. In a way, your writing can be even more descriptive than words with pictures because you can appeal to all the five senses through your words. Try out these ideas:

Smell

foul	musty
fragrant	dank
sweet	soapy
perfume	pungent
roses	moldy

Taste

heavy	thick
frothy	pasty
savory	grainy
gooey	

Sound

hiss	true
sweet	clatter

chatter	hum
buzz	growl
rubbing	

Touch

slippery	rough
satiny	coarse
smooth	grainy
velvety	bristly
silky	furry

You can use your visual or sensual thinking to bring your writing alive through the use of apt, interesting metaphors. A metaphor is a description of one thing through comparing it with something else. Sometimes you create the comparison in an explicit way through the use of the words *like* or *as*. This type of metaphor is called a *simile*. Here is an example of a simile:

His hair was like a bunch of wild straw.

But you can also make the comparison in a more subtle way, without the use of like or as:

When he woke up, his hair was a rumpled mess. The wild straw stuck up all over his head.

The following list contains metaphorical comparisons from actual young-adult novels. See what interesting comparisons you can imagine and write in your own story.

hail	ice marbles
chicks	red bundles
hair	wild halo
music	silver stream
voice	deep rolling river
stomach	sick tiger

guitar	dance partner
sweater	muted rainbow
city square	welcome mat

You will need different visual images depending on the type of young adult novel you write. Here is a list of several popular types of stories with some of the visual words that may help you bring the story alive.

Horse Story

mane	stirrups
roan	boots
palomino	jodhpurs
Western saddle	switch
pommel	corral
blanket	show ring
painter	tack

Sports Story

pinstripe uniform	Astroturf
chain-link fence	shoulder pads
metal bat	cleats
wooden bat	catcher's mask
baseball seams	chin guard
jersey	high-top sneakers
goal posts	

Inner-City Story

peeling paint	underpass
storefront	elevator
boarded-up window	laundry room
Dumpster	security-guard desk
candy store	gold teeth
graffiti	gold jewelry
subway car	park bench

Ballet Story

barre
mirror
slipper
toe shoe
upright piano
rehearsal skirt
tutu
leotard

tights
dance bag
hair band
wooden floor
jazz shoes
tulle
leggings

Camp Story

campfire
lake front
raft
rowboat
swimming trunks
bikini

mountain
rocks
cabin (bunk)
wire-mesh screen
mud
gnats

If you write for older readers, your leading characters will likely have different physical characteristics than those of their younger counterparts. Here are a few such features to imagine as you write.

Facial Hair

mustache
goatee
vandyke

sideburns
mutton chops

Piercing

eyebrow
nostril

tongue
lip

Attire

bra
jockstrap

hose
bikini

| muscle shirt | high heels |
| spandex pants | |

Outlandish Clothes

spiked collar	chains
leather pants	fishnet stockings
baggy pants	

No matter what age your audience, the important thing is to picture the scene you want to write. Whether writing for picture-book-age children or for young adults, write out the scene in words. Be as detailed as you can. These words may become an important guide to the illustrator of your picture book. For your YA reader, the words will be an important aspect of your book's appeal as you provide verbal clues that will allow young people to glean meaning from language.

Appendix

Resources for the Writer

The most important thing a children's book writer can do is read, read, read and get involved in activities for children's book writers. In this section, we provide a bibliography of wonderful children's books for you to read, as well as books to enrich your adult perspective.

First are examples of the many different types of children's books discussed in the earlier chapters. You can gain invaluable insights for your own work by reading these books with an eye toward the age of the reader, the format and the spark of genius that makes each book special and important. Try to analyze each book in light of the different considerations we have discussed: idea, format, character, setting, plot, writing and visual thinking.

Children's Books

Baby and Novelty Books

Pat the Bunny by Dorothy Kunhardt

What Is Hanukkah? by Harriet Ziefert

The Little Fur Family by Margaret Wise Brown

Where's Spot? by Eric Hill

The Cajun Gingerbread Boy by Berthe Amoss

Melly's Menorah by Amye Rosenberg

Pet the Baby Farm Animals, illustrated by Lucinda McQueen

Five Fairy-Tale Princesses by Berthe Amoss

All Aboard! by Chris L. Demarest

Picture Books

Goodnight Moon by Margaret Wise Brown

The Little Bookroom by Eleanor Farjeon

Little Tim and the Brave Sea Captain by Edward Ardizzone

The Tale of Peter Rabbit by Beatrix Potter

Harold and the Purple Crayon by Crockett Johnson

The Important Book by Margaret Wise Brown

The Runaway Bunny by Margaret Wise Brown

A Hole Is to Dig by Ruth Krauss

Where the Wild Things Are by Maurice Sendak

Noah's Ark by Peter Spier

Millions of Cats by Wanda Gag

Madeline by Ludwig Bemelmans

The Polar Express by Chris Van Allsburg

Curious George by H.A. Rey

Prayer for a Child by Rachel Field

The Story of Babar by Jean de Brunhoff

The Nutshell Library by Maurice Sendak

The Sorcerer's Apprentice by Nancy Willard

Tuesday by David Wiesner

Mirette on the High Wire by Emily Arnold McCully

The Napping House by Don and Audrey Wood

Have You Seen My Duckling? by Nancy Tafuri

Feathers for Lunch by Lois Ehlert

The Wheel on the Chimney by Margaret Wise Brown

Mister Dog by Margaret Wise Brown

Beauty and the Beast by Marianna Mayer

Just Me and My Dad by Mercer Mayer

Eloise by Kay Thompson

Frog Went a-Courtin' by John Langstaff

Like Jake and Me by Mavis Jukes

Bently and Egg by William Joyce

Amazing Grace by Mary Hoffman

Emily by Michael Bedard

The Bee Tree by Patricia Polacco

The Chicken Book by Garth Williams

How Much Is a Million? by David M. Schwartz

Starry Messenger by Peter Sis

A Visit to William Blake's Inn by Nancy Willard

The Five Chinese Brothers by Claire H. Bishop and Kurt Wiese

The Biggest Bear by Lynd Ward

The Animal Family by Randall Jarrell

Pish, Posh, Said Hieronymus Bosch by Nancy Willard

The Stupids Die by Harry Allard and James Marshall

Officer Buckle and Gloria by Peggy Rathmann

Stellaluna by Janell Cannon

No, David! by David Shannon

For Beginning Readers

Amelia Bedelia by Peggy Parish

Beethoven Lives Upstairs by Barbara Nichol

A Light in the Attic by Shel Silverstein

A Pizza the Size of the Sun by Jack Prelutsky

Zlateh the Goat by Isaac Bashevis Singer

A Birthday for Frances by Lillian and Russell Hoban

Frog and Toad Are Friends by Arnold Lobel

The Cat in the Hat by Dr. Seuss

Henry and Mudge by Cynthia Rylant

Johnny Germ Head by James Quigley

For Young Adults

The House of Sixty Fathers by Meindert de Jong

Charlotte's Web by E.B. White

The Court of the Stone Children by Eleanor Cameron

The Tombs of Atuan by Ursula K. LeGuin

A Wrinkle in Time by Madeleine L'Engle

Number the Stars by Lois Lowry

Forever by Judy Blume

Shiloh by Phyllis Reynolds Naylor

Sarah, Plain and Tall by Patricia MacLachlan

Where the Red Fern Grows by Wilson Rawls

A Day No Pigs Would Die by Robert Newton Peck

Invincible Louisa by Cornelia Meigs

The Chocolate War by Robert Cormier

Are You in the House Alone? by Richard Peck

Bard of Avon: The Story of William Shakespeare by Diane Stanley

Hiding to Survive by Maxine B. Rosenberg

Dominique Moceanu, as told to Steve Woodward

Freedom's Children: Young Civil Rights Activists Tell Their Own Stories by Ellen Levine

Oddballs by William Sleator

The Hero and the Crown by Robin McKinley

Many Waters by Madeleine L'Engle

Rabbit Hill by Robert Lawson

M.C. Higgins the Great by Virginia Hamilton

There's a Boy in the Girls' Bathroom by Louis Sachar

Dancing on the Edge by Han Nolan

The Adventures of Midnight Son by Denise Lewis Patrick

Classics

Each book on the following list has stood the test of time and is assured a place in the pantheon of great books for young people. These books provide the writer with the ultimate point of aspiration through extraordinary breadth of imagination, unforgettable characters, scintillating writing and that spark of true inspiration that makes a book a living thing.

Robinson Crusoe by Daniel Defoe

Gulliver's Travels by Jonathan Swift

Grimm's Popular Stories in English, translated by Edgar Taylor

A Christmas Carol by Charles Dickens

Fairy Tales by Hans Christian Andersen

Alice's Adventures in Wonderland by Lewis Carroll

Little Women by Louisa May Alcott

Treasure Island by Robert Louis Stevenson

A Child's Garden of Verses by Robert Louis Stevenson

The Adventures of Tom Sawyer by Mark Twain

Robin Hood by Howard Pyle

Heidi by Johanna Spyri

The Adventures of Huckleberry Finn by Mark Twain

The Jungle Book by Rudyard Kipling

Just-So Stories by Rudyard Kipling

The Nutcracker by E.T.A. Hoffmann

A Book of Nonsense by Edward Lear

Songs of Innocence and Songs of Experience by William Blake

The Diary of a Young Girl by Anne Frank

The Yearling by Marjorie Kinnan Rawlings

The Princess and Curdie by George MacDonald

The Wind in the Willows by Kenneth Grahame

Winnie-the-Pooh by A.A. Milne

The following books are ones that are resources for you, the adult writing for children. The books are organized by category and provide you with guidance about writing, enriching perspectives on children's literature, information about writer's conferences and work-shops, and good advice about getting published. Good luck!

Books About Writing Children's Books

Writing for Children and Young People by Lyn Wynham

Writing for Children by Ellen Roberts

Writing With Pictures by Uri Shulevitz

The Way to Write for Children by Joan Aiken

How to Write and Illustrate Children's Books and Get Them Published by Treld Pelkey, Treld Beckinell and Felicity Trotman

You Can Write Children's Books by Tracey E. Dils

Writing for Young Adults by Sherry Garland

Teach Yourself Writing for Children by Allen Frevin Jones and Lesley Pollinger

How to Write and Sell Children's Picture Books by Jean E. Karl

Writing and Publishing Books for Children in the 1990s by Olga Litowinsky

Children's Writer's Word Book by Alijandra Mogilner

Writing for Children by Catherine Woolley

Writing for Children and Teenagers by Lee Wyndham and Arnold Madison

Books About Children's Books

The Uses of Enchantment by Bruno Bettelheim

Books: Children and Men by Paul Hazard

Children's Books in England by F.J. Harvey Darton

The Classic Fairy Tales by Iona and Peter Opie

The Annotated Mother Goose by William Baring-Gould

Three Centuries of Books in Europe by Bettina Hurlimann

Children and Literature by John Warren Stewig

The Arbuthnot Anthology of Children's Literature by May Hill Arbuthnot

Picture-Book World by Bettina Hurlimann

The Art of Art for Children's Books by Diana Klemin

The Illustrated Book by Diana Klemin

Illustrators of Children's Books by Mahoney and Viguers

American Picturebooks from Noah's Ark to the Beast Within by Barbara Bader

The Telling Line by Douglas Martin

Children & Books by Zena Sutherland

Literature and the Child by John Warren Stewig

The Oxford Companion to Children's Literature by Humphrey Carpenter and Mari Prichard

The Making of Goodnight Moon by Leonard S. Marcus

The Oxford Dictionary of Nursery Rhymes, edited by Iona and Peter Opie

Should We Burn Babar? by Herbert Kohl

Books to Build On, edited by John Holdren and E.D. Hirsch, Jr.

Literacy Through the Book Arts by Paul Johnson

Creative Storytelling by Jack Zipes

The Case of Peter Rabbit by Margaret MacKey

Classics to Read Aloud to Your Children by William F. Russell

Good Stuff: Learning Tools for All Ages by Rebecca Rupp

The Literature Connection by Liz Rothlein and Anita Meyer Meinbach

Black Books Galore! by Donna Rand, Toni Trent Parker and Sheila Foster

A Child's Delight by Noel Perrin

Great Books for Boys by Kathleen O'Dean

Great Books for Girls by Kathleen O'Dean

The Pleasures of Children's Literature by Perry Nodelman

100 Books for Girls to Grow On by Shireen Dodson

Worlds of Childhood, edited by William Zinsser and Maurice Sendak

The Riverside Anthology of Children's Literature by Judith Saltman

Inside Picture Books by Ellen Handler Spitz

Books by and about Children's Book Authors

A Circle of Quiet by Madeleine L'Engle

A Girl From Mayhill by Beverly Cleary

Surprised by Joy by C.S. Lewis

The Enchanted Places by Christopher Milne

A History of the Writings of Beatrix Potter by Leslie Linder

Boy by Roald Dahl

Dear Genius: The Letters of Ursula Nordstrom by Leonard S. Marcus

A Caldecott Celebration by Leonard S. Marcus

The Abracadabra Kid: A Writer's Life by Sid Fleischman

No Pretty Pictures: A Child of War by Anita Lobel

Books About Writers' Conferences and Workshops

The Complete Guide to Writers' Conferences and Workshops by William Noble

Networking at Writer's Conferences by Steven D. Spratt and Lee G. Spratt

The Writing Workshop by Alan Ziegler

Books for Good Writing

The Elements of Style by William Strunk, Jr., and E.B. White

The Elements of Grammar by Margaret D. Shertzer

The Elements of Editing by Arthur Plotnik

The Chicago Manual of Style

Words Into Type by Marjorie E. Skillin and Robert M. Gay

Webster's Tenth New Collegiate Dictionary

Only Connect by Sheila Egoff

Telling Writing by Ken MacRorie

Books About Publishing

Business and Legal Forms for Authors and Self-Publishers by Tad Crawford

How to Be Your Own Literary Agent by Richard Curtis

Kirsch's Handbook of Publishing Law by Jonathan Kirsch

A Writer's Guide to Book Publishing by Richard Balkin

The Writer's Legal Companion by Brad Bunnin and Peter Beren

The Writer's Legal Guide by Tad Crawford and Tony Lyons

Literary Agents: A Writer's Introduction by John F. Baker

Children's Writer's & Illustrator's Market edited by Alice Pope

The Society of Children's Book Writers and Illustrators is a helpful organization that provides grassroots support for aspiring creators of books for young readers. The SCBWI also distributes helpful publications about the publishing process, including information about different editors and publishing companies. Contact your local chapter for support and answers to your questions.

Happy writing!

Index